The Mirror
of Dharma

Suggested study or reading order for beginners of books by Venerable Geshe Kelsang Gyatso Rinpoche

How to Transform Your Life
How to Understand the Mind
Joyful Path of Good Fortune
The Mirror of Dharma
The New Heart of Wisdom
Modern Buddhism
Tantric Grounds and Paths
The New Guide to Dakini Land
Essence of Vajrayana
The Oral Instructions of Mahamudra
Great Treasury of Merit
The New Eight Steps to Happiness
Introduction to Buddhism
How to Solve Our Human Problems
Meaningful to Behold
The Bodhisattva Vow
Universal Compassion
The New Meditation Handbook
Living Meaningfully, Dying Joyfully
Ocean of Nectar
Heart Jewel
Clear Light of Bliss
Mahamudra Tantra

This book is published under the auspices of the
NKT-IKBU International Temples Project
and the profit from its sale is designated for public
benefit through this fund.
[Reg. Charity number 1015054 (England)]
Find out more:
tharpa.com/benefit-all-world-peace

VENERABLE GESHE KELSANG
GYATSO RINPOCHE

The Mirror of Dharma

HOW TO FIND THE REAL MEANING OF HUMAN LIFE

THARPA PUBLICATIONS
UK • US • CANADA
AUSTRALIA • ASIA

First edition 2018

The right of Geshe Kelsang Gyatso
to be identified as author of this work
has been asserted by him in accordance with
the Copyright, Designs, and Patents Act 1988.

Tharpa Publications UK
Conishead Priory
Ulverston, Cumbria
LA12 9QQ, UK

Tharpa Publications US
47 Sweeney Road
Glen Spey, NY 12737
USA

There are Tharpa Publications offices around the world,
and Tharpa books are published in most major languages.
See pages 301-302 for contact details.

Library of Congress Control Number: 2018935671

British Library Cataloguing in Publication Data
A catalogue record for this book is
available from the British Library.

ISBN 978-1-910368-80-0 – paperback
ISBN 978-1-910368-81-7 – ePub
ISBN 978-1-910368-82-4 – kindle

Set in Palatino by Tharpa Publications.
Printed and bound in the United Kingdom by Bell and Bain Ltd.

Paper supplied from well-managed forests and other controlled
sources, and certified in accordance with the rules of the
Forest Stewardship Council.

Contents

Illustrations

PART ONE

Training in Contemplation

Buddha Shakyamuni

Introduction

The explanation given in this chapter will bring great benefit to those wishing to practise the very profound and blessed instructions presented in the following chapters. The subject of this book is how to put Buddha's teachings, or Dharma, into practice.

The first point we should think about is, 'Why do we need to practise Buddha's teachings?' The answer is very simple. It is because we want to be happy all the time, and we can fulfil this wish only by putting Buddha's teachings into practice. We therefore need to practise Buddha's teachings, Dharma, sincerely and purely.

Although we normally want to be happy all the time, even during sleep, we do not know how to do this. If someone were to ask us how to do this, we would have no clear answer. Do you have a clear answer? Some people may say, 'I will be happy all the time if I become wealthy, enjoy a good reputation and have the opportunity of a relationship with the person I desire.' I am very sorry, but this is not true! We can see that people who have all these things also experience great unhappiness and many problems. Many wealthy people and those in high positions experience great suffering and many dangers. We see and hear news about such things all the time.

Also, we should know that when, for example, we enjoy a holiday we may feel happy, but this enjoyment is not real happiness; it is just a reduction of our previous problems. If the happiness we experience by going on holiday were real happiness, it would follow that the holiday itself would be a real cause of happiness. But this is not true because, as we know, holidays can also cause many problems. We can apply this to other enjoyments, such as eating, drinking and sex. For example, if the happiness we experience from eating were real happiness, it would follow that eating in itself would be a real cause of happiness. If this were so then the more and more we ate without stopping, the more our happiness would increase. But in fact the opposite is true. Through this we can understand that in this impure world no-one has real happiness and freedom. This is because everybody seeks happiness from the wrong objects, and everybody experiences the problems of uncontrolled desire and ignorance.

The only way we can make ourself and others happy all the time is through practising Buddha's teachings. This is because happiness depends on a peaceful mind. Through practising Buddha's teachings we can develop and maintain a peaceful mind all the time, so that we will be happy all the time; regardless of whether our external conditions are good or bad, if we maintain a peaceful mind all the time we will be happy all the time.

We should know that right now we have a human life and we have met Buddhadharma. Through putting Buddha's teachings into practice we have the opportunity to maintain a peaceful mind all the time throughout our life, and in life after life. This is a wonderful and precious opportunity, which we should never waste. Understanding this we should encourage ourself to practise Buddha's teachings, Dharma, purely and sincerely. In this way we should guide ourself to the spiritual path, which gives us great meaning in this life and in life after life. Only Buddha's teachings, Dharma, are the real method to make ourself and others happy all the time, not only in this life but also in countless future lives. Therefore they are the source of all happiness.

We should also think, 'Why do I need to be concerned for my future lives?' We need to be concerned for our future lives because the happiness and freedom of our future lives are more important than those of this life. Our present life is just one single life. If we died today it would end today, but our future lives are countless and endless. We know that most people are concerned only with this life, not with future lives, and therefore they neglect the happiness and freedom of their countless future lives. This is because they do not understand about the existence of future lives.

If we understood the nature and function of our mind correctly we would clearly understand the existence of our future lives. We often say, 'My mind, my mind', but if someone were to ask us 'What is your mind?' we would have no correct answer. This is because we do not understand the nature and function of the mind correctly. The mind is by nature something that is empty like space, always lacking form, shape and colour. The mind is not actual space because produced space possesses shape and colour. During the day it can be light and during the night it can be dark, but mind never possesses shape and colour.

The mind is empty, but it is not correct to say that the mind is emptiness. What is the difference between empty and emptiness? In Buddhism, emptiness has great meaning. It is the real nature of things, and is a very profound and meaningful object. If we realize emptiness directly we will attain permanent liberation from all the sufferings of this life and our countless future lives; there is no greater meaning than this. So emptiness is a very meaningful object, but empty is just empty – it has no special meaning. Therefore, we say that the mind is empty, which means that it always lacks form, shape and colour; and we say that space is empty, which means that it lacks obstructive contact. And when we say, 'My purse is empty', this means that there is no money inside it. Through this we understand that empty and emptiness have very different meanings.

The function of the mind is to perceive or understand objects. We normally say, 'I see such and such'; this is because our mind sees that object. Because our mind understands things we say, 'I understand.' So our perception and understanding of objects are functions of our mind; without mind we are powerless to perceive and understand them.

Another main function of the mind is to impute things. Without a name things cannot exist. Names are imputed by mind through thinking, 'This is this'. So things exist only because mind imputes them. Through this we can understand that everything including the world is created by mind. There is no creator other than mind. This truth is not difficult to understand if we examine it with a positive mind.

Thus, in summary, the mind is something whose nature is empty like space, always lacking form, shape and colour, and whose function is to perceive or understand objects. Through understanding the nature and function of the mind correctly we can understand that our mind is completely different from our body, and this proves that after our death, although our body will cease, our mind will not. The mind leaves the body and goes to the next life like a bird leaving one nest and moving to another. Or, for example, during sleep when we are dreaming our body remains on our bed while our mind goes out to the dream world and sees and experiences so many different dream objects. This shows that when we die our body will remain in this world but our mind will go to its next life and, like a dream, see and experience so many different things of its next life. Through understanding this we will have no doubts about the existence of future lives.

Immediately after our death we will possess a new body, the body of an intermediate state being, a living being who is between its past life and its next rebirth. Generally the life span of intermediate state beings is only forty-nine days. Within that time they will take their next rebirth as a human being, god or demi-god, or in lower realms as an animal, hungry ghost or hell being. If we are born as a human being we have to experience human suffering, and if we are born as an animal we have to experience animal suffering, and so forth.

We should know that we have taken rebirth as a human being in this world because in our previous lives we per-formed contaminated virtuous actions that caused us to be born in this impure world as a human being. This is why we are here. No-one sent us to this world saying, 'You should go and live in the human world.' In the same way animals have taken rebirth as an animal in their own realm because in their previous lives they performed non-virtuous actions that were the main cause of their taking that rebirth.

No-one has the power or authority to say to living beings, 'You should go to the human realm, the animal realm, the hell realm, or the god realm.' Because of our previous different actions, or karma, accumulated since beginningless time we all take different rebirths and experience different sufferings.

Buddha gave detailed explanations through which we can understand the connection between our actions performed in previous lives, either virtuous or non-virtuous, and our experiences in this life, either happiness or suffering.

To prove this connection Buddha also gave many examples. There was once a man called Shri Datta who committed many extremely negative actions. Later, when he was old, Shri Datta requested Buddha to grant him ordination. It is said that to receive ordination we need at least some small virtuous potential within our mental continuum that is a cause of liberation, the supreme permanent inner peace called 'nirvana'; but when clairvoyant disciples of Buddha examined Shri Datta they were unable to find a single such potential and so they declared him unfit for ordination. However, these disciples could not see the subtle karmic potentials that are seen only by enlightened beings. When Buddha looked into Shri Datta's dark mind he saw a tiny potential for virtue. He told his disciples, 'Many aeons ago Shri Datta was a fly who landed on some horse dung near a stupa of Buddha. It was raining heavily and the water carried the dung, together with the fly, around the stupa. Although the fly had no intention of circumambulating the stupa, it nevertheless received Buddha's blessings just by seeing the stupa, and this left on its mind a virtuous potential to attain liberation.' Buddha then granted him ordination. As a result, Shri Datta's virtuous potentials increased and he attained liberation in that lifetime.

In the Lamrim instructions it says that just seeing an image of a Buddha places in our mind a potential or mental imprint that is a cause of enlightenment. This is because Buddhas are completely pure, beyond the cycle of impure life, samsara. This potential is inside our impure mind; although the container, our mind, is impure, its content, the potential that comes from just seeing an image of Buddha, is always pure. This potential will give us great meaning, as we can understand from the story of Shri Datta.

Another question we need to ask ourself is, 'Why do we need permanent liberation from suffering?' It is because temporary liberation from a particular suffering is not enough; even animals can have such a liberation. At the moment we may be free from physical suffering and mental pain, but this is only temporary. Later in this life and in our countless future lives we will have to experience unbearable physical suffering and mental pain again and again without end. Therefore there is no doubt that we need to attain permanent liberation from all the sufferings of this life and our countless future lives. In Buddhism, this permanent liberation is called 'nirvana'. We can attain this liberation only through practising Buddha's teachings, principally his teachings on selflessness, or emptiness. An essential explanation of emptiness is given in Part Two of this book in the section *Training in Meditation on Emptiness*, and an extensive explanation can be found in the book *Modern Buddhism*.

Buddha's teachings, or Dharma, are the practical method to find the real meaning of human life. Because Dharma is very profound, when we are reading Dharma books we should contemplate their meaning again and again until it touches our heart. This is very important for everyone.

Essential Insights into
The Three Principal Aspects
of the Path to Enlightenment

Je Tsongkhapa gave the instructions of *The Three Principal Aspects of the Path to Enlightenment* as advice from his heart. I will give an essential commentary to these instructions.

WHO IS JE TSONGKHAPA?

From the point of view of common appearance Je Tsongkhapa was a Tibetan Buddhist Master and scholar, and the founder of the New Kadampa lineage. The Indian Buddhist Master Atisha founded the Kadampa lineage in general, and Je Tsongkhapa founded the New Kadampa lineage in particular. Both lineages are the very essence of Buddha's teachings and are most suitable for people of this modern age.

In truth, Je Tsongkhapa is an emanation of Buddha Shakyamuni, the founder of Buddhism. Buddha emanates as Je Tsongkhapa to spread his pure teachings of Sutra and Tantra in general, and especially Highest Yoga Tantra, throughout the world. In the 'Prediction' chapter of *King*

Je Tsongkhapa

of Instructions Sutra Buddha gave a prediction about Je Tsongkhapa. He used Je Tsongkhapa's actual name, Losang Dragpa, Sumati Kirti in Sanskrit, and the name of the monastery, Ganden, which Je Tsongkhapa founded not far from Lhasa; and he explained how Losang Dragpa would clarify Buddha's teachings of Sutra and Tantra to prevent people from following mistaken views. This prediction indicates that in truth Buddha himself emanates as Je Tsongkhapa to spread his doctrine throughout the world.

In the *Ganden Emanation Scripture* the Wisdom Buddha Manjushri said:

Tsongkhapa, crown ornament of the scholars of the
Land of the Snows,
You are Buddha Shakyamuni and Vajradhara, the
source of all attainments,
Avalokiteshvara, the treasury of unobservable
compassion,
Manjushri, the supreme stainless wisdom,
And Vajrapani, the destroyer of the hosts of maras.
O Venerable Guru-Buddha, synthesis of all Three
Jewels,
With my body, speech and mind, respectfully I make
requests:
Please grant your blessings to ripen and liberate
myself and others,
And bestow the common and supreme attainments.

This request prayer to Je Tsongkhapa proves that Je Tsongkhapa is the manifestation of Buddha Shakyamuni, Buddha Vajradhara, Avalokiteshvara, the Buddha of

Compassion, Manjushri, the Buddha of Wisdom, and Vajrapani, the Buddha of Power. This in turn proves that he is the manifestation of all the Buddhas. Thus, if we sincerely rely on Je Tsongkhapa and put his oral instructions into practice with strong faith, we will attain enlightenment very quickly. The great practitioner Gyalwa Ensapa and many of his followers attained enlightenment within three years through sincerely practising the oral instructions of Je Tsongkhapa. This is magical!

Many scholars have said that the power of Je Tsongkhapa's blessings and his skilful methods to lead practitioners to the state of enlightenment is unequalled among those of all other Buddhas. We should rejoice in having met the doctrine of Je Tsongkhapa, and in having the opportunity to listen to and practise the oral instructions of this precious Guru who is the synthesis of all Buddhas.

THE ACTUAL EXPLANATION OF THE ESSENTIAL INSIGHTS INTO *THE THREE PRINCIPAL ASPECTS OF THE PATH TO ENLIGHTENMENT*

In the root text Je Tsongkhapa says:

I will explain to the best of my ability
The essential meaning of the teachings of all the
    Buddhas [renunciation],
The main path of the Bodhisattvas, who have
    compassion for all living beings [bodhichitta],
And the ultimate path of the fortunate ones who are
    seeking liberation [the correct view of emptiness].

You should not be attached to worldly enjoyments,
But strive to find the real meaning of human life
By listening to and practising the instructions given
    here,
Which all the previous Buddhas practised with
    delight.

In this stage, through contemplating the meaning of these verses, we generate a feeling of happiness at receiving these precious instructions and advice from Je Tsongkhapa's heart, and we make the strong determination to put these instructions into practice.

We should know that in this impure world there is no real happiness at all. The happiness that comes from worldly enjoyments is not real happiness but only a reduction of our previous problems. Understanding this we should develop a sincere wish to attain the supreme happiness of enlightenment, which is the real meaning of human life. As human beings only we can achieve this. The moment we attain enlightenment we have the ability to benefit each and every living being every day through our blessings and our countless emanations. Enlightenment is the inner light of wisdom that is permanently free from all mistaken appearance and whose function is to bestow mental peace, the source of happiness, on each and every living being every day. The method for attaining enlightenment is renunciation, bodhichitta and the correct view of emptiness, which are the paths to enlightenment, known as the 'three principal aspects of the path to enlightenment'.

RENUNCIATION

Renunciation does not mean that we abandon our family and friends, and become isolated from people. In Buddhism renunciation is a part of wisdom – a wisdom that gives us great encouragement to liberate ourself permanently from lower rebirth, from rebirth in the cycle of impure life, samsara, or from a rebirth in which we possess a self-cherishing mind. We need this wisdom, which leads us to the correct path to our finding the real meaning of human life.

The second line of the first verse of the root text says that renunciation is *'The essential meaning of the teachings of all the Buddhas.'* How can we understand this? In *Expressing the Names of Manjushri Tantra* Buddha said that although there are renunciations of the three paths the final result is only one. Renunciations of the three paths are renunciation that spontaneously wishes to liberate ourself permanently from lower rebirth, renunciation that spontaneously wishes to liberate ourself permanently from samsaric rebirth, and renunciation that spontaneously wishes to liberate ourself permanently from a rebirth in which we possess self-cherishing. The first renunciation is renunciation of the path of a person of initial scope, the second is renunciation of the path of a person of middling scope and the third is renunciation of the path of a person of great scope. This proves that renunciation is very important to begin, make progress on and complete the path to enlightenment, which in turn proves that renunciation is the essential meaning of the teachings of all the Buddhas. Although there are renunciations of the three paths the final result is only one, the attainment of enlightenment.

HOW TO DEVELOP PURE RENUNCIATION

The root text says:

> Attachment to the fulfilment of your own wishes,
>   uncontrolled desire,
> Is the main cause of all your own problems and
>   suffering,
> And there is no method to abandon it without first
>   developing renunciation.
> Thus you should apply great effort to develop and
>   maintain pure renunciation.
>
> When, through daily training, you develop the
>   spontaneous thoughts:
> 'I may die today' and 'A precious human life is so
>   rare',
> And you meditate on the truth of karma and the
>   sufferings of the cycle of impure life, samsara,
> Your attachment to worldly enjoyments will cease.
>
> In this way, when uncontrolled desire for worldly
>   enjoyments
> Does not arise even for a moment,
> But a mind longing for liberation, nirvana, arises
>   throughout the day and the night,
> At that time pure renunciation is generated.

The explanation in the root text on how to generate pure renunciation is the same as explained by Je Tsongkhapa in his Lamrim teachings, and I also explain this in detail in the book *Modern Buddhism*. Based on oral instructions we can also practise the following. We imagine and think:

Today as a human being I enjoy human conditions and tonight I go to sleep as a human being, but during sleep due to karma and other circumstances my breathing stops completely. Then tomorrow, instead of waking up as a human being, I reach a place pervaded by fire, and my body becomes inseparable from fire. I am reborn in hell, where I will experience unbearable pain for millions of years.

Contemplating this imagination, which comes from our wisdom, again and again, we will develop fear of samsaric rebirth in general and of lower rebirth in particular. This fear is renunciation, which comes from our wisdom. We meditate on this renunciation continually until we maintain this fear day and night without ever forgetting it. At this time we have developed pure renunciation, or renunciation of the path. Path in this context is a spiritual path or spiritual realization. The effectiveness of this meditation depends on our potential for spiritual realizations.

BODHICHITTA

'Bodhi' means enlightenment and 'chitta' means mind. Bodhichitta is a mind that spontaneously wishes to attain enlightenment to benefit each and every living being every day. It is the gateway through which we enter the path to enlightenment, and the supreme good heart of the Sons and Daughters of the Conqueror Buddhas, who are also called 'Bodhisattvas'. They will all soon become Buddhas, enlightened beings. We should follow their example. The moment we develop bodhichitta we will become a Son or Daughter of the Buddhas and we will soon become a Buddha. How wonderful!

HOW TO GENERATE THE PRECIOUS MIND OF BODHICHITTA

The root text says:

> However, if this renunciation is not maintained
> By the compassionate mind of bodhichitta,
> It will not be a cause of the unsurpassed happiness,
>   enlightenment;
> Therefore, you must apply effort to generate the
>   precious mind of bodhichitta.

Through contemplating the meaning of this verse, we make the determination to apply effort to generate the precious mind of bodhichitta based on the following verses:

> Swept along by the currents of the four powerful
>   rivers [birth, ageing, sickness and death],
> Tightly bound by the chains of karma so hard to
>   release,
> Ensnared within the iron net of self-grasping,
> Completely enveloped by the pitch-black darkness
>   of ignorance,
>
> Taking rebirth after rebirth in boundless samsara,
> And unceasingly tormented by the three sufferings
>   [painful feelings, changing suffering and
>   pervasive suffering] –

**Through contemplating the state of your mothers, all
living beings, in conditions such as these,
Generate the supreme mind of bodhichitta.**

In this practice there are five stages of contemplation and meditation. We first strongly recognize that all living beings are our mothers. In *The Condensed Perfection of Wisdom Sutra* Buddha said, 'You should recognize all living beings as your mothers or fathers and always help them with loving kindness and compassion.' We should keep this advice in our heart.

Because of our changing rebirths we do not recognize each other, and because of this we believe that there are many enemies and countless strangers. This is a mistaken belief and ignorance. In truth, all living beings are our mothers. In our countless former lives we took countless rebirths, and in each of these rebirths we had a mother and so we have countless mothers. Where are all these countless mothers now? They are all the living beings that are alive today. Understanding and thinking this, from our heart we strongly recognize that all living beings are our kind mothers and we cherish them, believing: 'They are more important than myself who am only one single person.'

With this cherishing love for all living beings we engage in the following practice. In the first stage we contemplate and deeply think how countless mother living beings are experiencing the cycle of the sufferings of birth, sickness, ageing and death, continually in life after life without end. We should remember the detailed explanation in the book *Modern Buddhism*. Then we generate a strong wish to liberate all of them permanently from this suffering. This wish is compassion for all living beings. To fulfil this wish we make the strong determination to attain enlightenment. This determination is the compassionate mind of bodhichitta. We then meditate on this determination continually until we maintain our determination day and night without ever forgetting it.

In the second stage we contemplate how all mother living beings are tightly bound by the chains of karma – the non-virtuous actions they have performed out of attachment, anger or ignorance, and that cause them never to be free from suffering and problems. We generate a sincere wish to release all of them from these chains permanently, which is compassion. To fulfil this wish we make the strong determination to attain enlightenment. This determination is bodhichitta. We then meditate on this determination continually until we maintain our determination day and night without ever forgetting it.

In the third stage, the root text says that living beings are ensnared within the iron net of self-grasping ignorance. In this context, the definition of self-grasping is a mind that mistakenly believes that ourself or others that we normally see or perceive actually exist. We should contemplate the meaning of this definition again and again until we clearly recognize our self-grasping ignorance, which always abides at our heart and whose function is to destroy our mental peace and happiness. With this recognition we contemplate that because each and every living being is ensnared within the iron net of self-grasping ignorance none of them has any real happiness. This is because their mental peace, the source of happiness, is always being destroyed by their self-grasping ignorance, which always remains in their hearts.

Understanding and thinking this we develop a sincere wish to give pure happiness to all living beings who are our mothers. To fulfil this wish we make a strong determination to attain enlightenment. This determination is bodhichitta. We meditate on this determination continually until we maintain our determination day and night without ever forgetting it.

In the fourth stage we contemplate that although each and every living being wishes to be happy all the time, and to be permanently free from every kind of problem and suffering, they do not know how to do this. This is because their minds are deeply covered by the thick darkness of ignorance not understanding the real nature of things. Whatever they see or perceive is a mistaken appearance, a hallucination. Understanding and thinking this we develop a sincere wish to liberate all living beings permanently from ignorance, a mind that mistakenly believes that the things we normally see actually exist. To fulfil this wish we make a strong determination to attain enlightenment. This determination is bodhichitta. We meditate on this determination continually until we maintain our determination day and night without ever forgetting it.

In the fifth stage we contemplate how each and every living being in life after life is wandering in samsara, the endless cycle of impure life, and is experiencing the sufferings of painful feelings, changing suffering and pervasive suffering, as explained in detail in the books *Joyful Path of Good Fortune* and *Great Treasury of Merit*. Through contemplating this again and again we develop a sincere wish to liberate all of them permanently from this suffering. To fulfil this wish we make a strong determination to attain enlightenment. This determination is bodhichitta. We meditate on this determination continually until we maintain our determination day and night without ever forgetting it.

The meaning of these explanations of the contemplations and meditations on both renunciation and bodhichitta is very clear. However, our normal problem is that our understanding remains only intellectual and does not touch our hearts, and because of this we achieve nothing. What we really need is to gain deep experience of these contemplations and meditations. Through this we need to change our mind, first into renunciation, then into cherishing love for all living beings, then into compassion for all living beings and then into bodhichitta. This is the advice from Je Tsongkhapa's heart.

THE CORRECT VIEW OF EMPTINESS

The wisdom that believes the things or phenomena we normally see or perceive do not exist is the correct view of emptiness. Because the object of this wisdom is emptiness, the mere absence of the things or phenomena we normally see or perceive, this wisdom is called the 'correct view of emptiness'. Only this view is the correct view through which we can attain permanent liberation from suffering and ignorance. The view believing the things we normally see or perceive actually exist is ignorance, the root of all suffering. In the *Perfection of Wisdom Sutra* Buddha says that if we search for things with wisdom we cannot find them. We cannot find our form, feelings, discriminations, compositional factors and consciousness. Thus we cannot find our self. This proves that the things we normally see do not exist. A detailed explanation of this can be found in the book *Modern Buddhism*.

If the things we normally see do not exist, then how do things really exist? Things exist in dependence on their mere name. If we are satisfied with their mere name, things exist. Beyond their mere name nothing exists at all.

To solve our daily problems we can practise as follows. From our heart we should understand and think, 'All the suffering, problems, difficulties, sickness, painful feelings, receiving harm, not finding things I desire and losing things I am attached to, experienced by myself that I normally see, do not exist. This is because myself that I normally see does not exist.' Understanding this and thinking deeply we can relax and remain with a peaceful mind all the time, so that we will be happy all the time. In this way, because we are happy all the time our own problems will all disappear.

There are three levels of the correct view of emptiness – according to Hinayana Sutras, according to Mahayana Sutras and according to the Vajrayana. The most supreme of these is the correct view of emptiness that Buddha explained in the Vajrayana. In Vajrayana, or Tantra, Buddha explained about the union of appearance and emptiness. The wisdom realizing this union is the correct view of emptiness, which is Buddha's ultimate view. The union of appearance and emptiness means that all phenomena – the appearance – and their emptiness are one object, not two objects. For example, our body – the appearance – and its emptiness are one object, not two objects. When we see our body, in truth we see only the emptiness of our body because the real nature of our body is its emptiness. However, we do not understand this because of our ignorance. We normally see our body as something that exists from its own side. This is mistaken appearance from which all suffering and problems develop endlessly. We should know that there is no 'our body' other than its emptiness. We should apply this knowledge to all other phenomena. To understand this subject of union correctly we need to be very patient. When, through correctly understanding and continually training in the union of appearance and emptiness, we directly experience the union of appearance and emptiness we will directly experience our environment, enjoyments, body and mind as the enlightened environment, enjoyments, body and mind, and we will directly experience ourself as an enlightened being – the union of Buddha, the union of Vajradhara, the union of Heruka, and so forth.

The root text says:

> **But even though you may be acquainted with renunciation and bodhichitta,**
> **If you do not possess the wisdom realizing the way things really are,**
> **You will not be able to cut the root of samsara,**
> **Therefore strive in the means for realizing dependent relationship.**

Je Tsongkhapa advises us saying, '*Therefore strive in the means for realizing dependent relationship.*' Dependent relationship is a very important subject. Through correctly understanding this we can understand the way things really are. The great scholar Aryadeva said,

> Just as the body sense power pervades the entire body,
> So ignorance pervades all delusions.

Thus, if we cut our ignorance by applying great
    effort to realize the real meaning of dependent
    relationship
All our delusions will cease.
Please keep this instruction in your heart.

Things exist in dependence on their causes and conditions, in dependence on their parts, in dependence on their basis of imputation and in dependence on their mere name. The last of these is subtle dependent relationship. When we realize subtle dependent relationship our understanding of emptiness is qualified. Things existing in dependence on their causes and conditions proves that things do not exist from their own side, and this in turn proves that the things we normally see or perceive do not exist. This in turn proves that things exist in dependence on their mere name, which is the real meaning of dependent relationship. The way things really exist is in dependence on their mere name. There are no things other than their mere name. This is subtle dependent relationship.

We should practise the following contemplation and meditation,

Things existing in dependence on their causes and conditions proves that they do not exist from their own side. This in turn proves that the things we normally see or perceive do not exist, and this in turn proves that things exist in dependence on their mere name. The way things really exist is in dependence on their mere name.

When through contemplating this again and again we realize clearly that the way things really exist is in dependence on their mere name, we hold this profound knowledge in our heart and meditate on it for as long as possible. Through continually practising this contemplation and meditation our self-grasping, the root of all suffering, will decrease and finally cease completely.

The root text says:

When you clearly see phenomena such as samsara and nirvana, and cause and effect, as they exist,
And at the same time you see that all the phenomena you normally see or perceive do not exist,
You have entered the path of the correct view of emptiness,
Thus delighting all the Buddhas.

In this stage we need to accomplish the following two things: (1) we need to negate the objects of negation of emptiness – the things and phenomena we normally see or perceive – and (2) we need to realize that the phenomena of samsara and nirvana, and cause and effect, all actually exist. When we accomplish these two without seeing any contradictions between them we have entered the path of the correct view of emptiness, thus delighting all the Buddhas.

The root text says:

If you perceive and believe that the appearance, phenomena,
And the empty, emptiness of phenomena,
Are dualistic,
You have not yet realized Buddha's intention.

With these words Je Tsongkhapa is saying that if we perceive and believe appearance and emptiness are dualistic we have not yet realized Buddha's intention. Thus we need to apply effort to realize Buddha's ultimate intention, which is to realize non-dual appearance and emptiness.

In general, all phenomena are included within two, appearance and emptiness. Phenomena themselves are appearance and their emptiness is empty. This appearance and empty are non-dual, which means one object not two. This is like the blue of the sky and the sky itself. The blue of the sky is the sky itself; there is no blue of the sky other than the sky itself – the sky itself appears as blue. Because the real nature of phenomena is the emptiness of phenomena, when we perceive phenomena in truth we perceive the emptiness of phenomena, but due to ignorance we cannot understand this. There are no phenomena other than their emptiness. Thus, phenomena – which is appearance – and their emptiness – which is empty – are non-dual, which means one object, not two. Through this explanation we can understand the meaning of non-dual appearance and empty. When, through mentally contemplating the meaning of this explanation again and again, we realize the non-dual appearance and empty as an endless space of emptiness, we hold this profound knowledge in our heart and meditate on it continually until it becomes the spontaneous realization of non-dual appearance and empty. Through this our dualistic appearance and mistaken appearance will cease and we will thus attain enlightenment quickly.

For qualified Tantric practitioners, in this endless space of emptiness their own environment, enjoyments, body, mind and their own self naturally appear as the enlightened environment, enjoyments, body, mind and self of an enlightened being, all naturally existing in dependence on their mere name.

The meaning of non-dual appearance and emptiness is very profound and not easy to understand. The wisdom that realizes non-dual appearance and emptiness is a higher level of the correct view of emptiness, and training in this wisdom is the quick path to enlightenment. Je Tsongkhapa took these instructions from the *Ganden Emanation Scripture*, whose nature is the wisdom of Buddha Manjushri.

If we have within ourself a strong potential for spiritual realizations, then with this condition we will easily develop and maintain profound knowledge and spiritual realizations. We can accomplish this condition, a strong potential for spiritual realizations, within ourself by sincerely practising the Guru yoga of the Wisdom Buddha Je Tsongkhapa. Through this we will receive the powerful blessings of all the Buddhas through our Guru so that we will easily develop and maintain profound knowledge and spiritual realizations. Practitioners such as Gyalwa Ensapa and his disciples and Je Sherab Senge and his disciples are witnesses to this. They attained the state of enlightenment within three years. This is magical. Through this we can understand how fortunate we are to have the opportunity to practise these instructions. There are two principal Guru yogas of Je Tsongkhapa: *Offering to the Spiritual Guide* and *The Hundreds of Deities of the Joyful Land*, which are both extracted from the *Ganden Emanation Scripture*. The practices of these two Guru yogas are powerful methods to grow our potential for attaining enlightenment quickly so that we can attain enlightenment quickly.

The root text says:

Through just seeing that things exist
In dependence on their mere name,
If your self-grasping reduces or ceases,
At that time you have completed your understanding
    of emptiness.

The meaning of this verse is very clear. At this stage we need to train in subtle dependent relationship – that phenomena exist in dependence on their mere name and not from their own side. This means that we need to contemplate and meditate on this subtle dependent relationship continually.

The root text says:

Moreover, if you negate the extreme of existence
By simply realizing that phenomena are just mere
    appearance,
And if you negate the extreme of non-existence
By simply realizing that all the phenomena you
    normally see or perceive do not exist,

And if you realize how, for example, the emptiness
    of cause and effect
Is perceived as cause and effect,
Because there is no cause and effect other than
    emptiness,
With these realizations you will not be harmed by
    extreme view.

Extreme view is very harmful for ourself and others. For this reason Je Tsongkhapa advises us to apply effort to develop the above realizations so that we will be free from this harmful view.

We should distinguish between extreme and extreme view. An extreme is something that is exaggerated and that actually does not exist, and an extreme view is a mistaken belief that exists in our mind. Phenomena existing from their own side is the extreme of existence, and phenomena completely non-existing is the extreme of non-existence. Neither of these extremes exists.

The root text says:

When, in this way, you have correctly realized the
**   essential points**
Of the three principal aspects of the path,
Dear One, withdraw into solitary retreat, generate
**   and maintain strong effort**
And quickly accomplish the final goal.

This is the final advice from Je Tsongkhapa's heart. We should keep this advice in our heart and put it into practice.

Guru Sumati Buddha Heruka

Request to the Lord of All Lineages

REQUEST PRAYER FOR PRACTISING LAMRIM – THE STAGES OF THE PATH TO ENLIGHTENMENT – LOJONG – TRAINING THE MIND – GENERATION STAGE AND COMPLETION STAGE

Concentrating on the meaning of this prayer, while being completely free from distractions, we engage in the following simple practice. We should memorize *Request to the Lord of All Lineages*, which is a very blessed prayer. We should mentally recite this prayer many times every day, even when relaxing or lying down, while concentrating on the meaning of each individual verse. Our understanding of the meaning of each verse should touch our heart, and through this our mind will transform into wisdom, cherishing love, compassion and so forth. There is no greater meaning than engaging in this practice. Please keep this advice in your heart.

First we imagine and think, 'In the space before me appears my root Guru in the aspect of Conqueror Losang Dragpa, Je Tsongkhapa. At his heart is Buddha Shakyamuni, and at his heart is Buddha Heruka. They are one person, known as Guru Sumati Buddha Heruka, but with different aspects.' We simply believe that Guru Sumati Buddha Heruka is actually present in front of us, and we then engage in the following request prayer:

O Venerable Conqueror Losang Dragpa,
Who are the Glorious Lord of all lineages, Heruka,
In whose single body all Buddhas, their worlds and
    their retinues abide,
I request you please bestow your blessings.

My kind, precious root Guru,
Who are inseparably one with Heruka,
In whose great bliss all phenomena are gathered into
    one,
I request you please bestow your blessings.

Since the root of all spiritual attainments
Is relying purely upon the Spiritual Guide,
Please now bestow the profound blessings of your
    body, speech and mind
Upon my body, speech and mind.

Out of his great kindness Je Tsongkhapa introduced
All the Sutra and Tantra teachings of Buddha as
    practical instructions.
However, my great good fortune in having met holy
    Dharma, the doctrine of Buddha,
Might remain with me for just this one life.

Yet my breath is like mist about to vanish
And my life is like a candle flame about to die in the
    wind.
Since there is no guarantee I will not die today,
Now is the only time to take the real meaning of
    human life, the attainment of enlightenment.

In my countless former lives I accumulated various
    kinds of non-virtuous action
And as a result I will have to experience the
    unbearable suffering of lower rebirth for many
    aeons.
Since this is unbearable for me, I sincerely seek refuge
In Buddha, Dharma and Sangha from the depths of
    my heart.

I will sincerely apply effort
To receiving Buddha's blessings,
Receiving help from Sangha, the pure spiritual
    practitioners,
And practising Dharma purely.

Through engaging in this practice continuously
I will accomplish the actual refuge in my mind –
The realizations of holy Dharma
That permanently liberate me from all suffering and
    problems.

The cause of suffering is non-virtuous actions
And the cause of happiness is virtuous actions.
Since this is completely true
I will definitely abandon the first and practise the
    second.

Like mistakenly believing
A poisonous drink to be nectar,
Attachment with grasping at objects of desire
Is the cause of great danger.

In the cycle of impure life, samsara,
There is no real protection from suffering.
Wherever I am born, either as a lower or higher being,
I will have to experience only suffering.

The flesh and bones of all the bodies I have previously
    taken if gathered together would be equal to Mount
    Meru,
And if the blood and bodily fluids were gathered they
    would be equal to the deepest ocean.
Although I have taken countless bodies as Brahma,
    Indra, chakravatin kings, gods and ordinary
    humans,
There has been no meaning from any of these, for still
    I continue to suffer.

If having been born in the hells drinking molten
    copper, as insects whose bodies turned into mud,
And as dogs, pigs and so forth who ate enough filth to
    cover the whole earth,
And if, as it is said, the tears I have shed from all this
    suffering are vaster than an ocean,
I still do not feel any sorrow or fear, do I have a mind
    made of iron?

Understanding this, I will make continuous effort to
    cease samsaric rebirth
By striving to permanently abandon its root,
    self-grasping ignorance.
In dependence upon this renunciation I will open the
    door to the path to liberation

And strive to practise the three higher trainings, the
synthesis of all paths.

With my mind like a fine horse heading for higher
ground
Guided by the reins of the Dharma of the three higher
trainings,
And urged onwards with the whip of strong effort,
Now I will swiftly travel the path to liberation.

All mother living beings who care for me with such
kindness
Are drowning in the fearful ocean of samsara.
If I give no thought to their pitiful suffering
I am like a mean and heartless child.

Since throughout my beginningless lives until now, the
root of all my suffering has been my self-cherishing
mind,
I must expel it from my heart, cast it afar and cherish
only other living beings.
Thus, I will complete my practice of exchanging self
with others.
O my precious Guru, please bestow your blessings so
that I may complete this profound practice.

To permanently liberate all mother living beings
From suffering and mistaken appearance,
I will attain the Union of the state of enlightenment
Through the practice of the six perfections.

Eliminating the distractions of my mind completely,
Observing and holding a single object of meditation
    with mindfulness,
And preventing the obstacles of mental sinking and
    mental excitement from arising,
In this way I will control my mind with clear and
    joyful meditation.

All my appearances in dreams teach me
That all my appearances when awake do not exist;
Thus for me all my dream appearances
Are the supreme instructions of my Guru.

The phenomena that I normally see or perceive
Are deceptive – created by mistaken minds.
If I search for the reality of what I see,
There is nothing there that exists – I perceive only
    empty like space.

When I search with my wisdom eye,
All the things that I normally see disappear
And only their mere name remains.
With this mere name I simply accept everything for
    the purpose of communicating with others.

The way phenomena exist is just this.
Guru Father Je Tsongkhapa clarified this following
    Nagarjuna's intention.
Thus, the correct view of emptiness free from the two
    extremes
Is extremely profound.

With my having experience of the common paths,
The principal of Akanishta Pure Land, Vajradhara
    Heruka,
Now appears in this world as an emanation of
    Heruka
In the form of my root Guru
Who has led me inside the great mandala of the body
    of Heruka
And granted me the four empowerments to ripen my
    mental continuum.
Thus I have become a great fortunate one who has the
    opportunity to accomplish in this life
The Union of Heruka by accomplishing No More
    Learning, the state of enlightenment.

The kindness of Guru Heruka Father and Mother is
    inconceivable
And the kindness of my root Guru is inconceivable.
Because of this good fortune and through the power of
    my correct imagination
I now abide in the great mandala of Heruka, the
    nature of my purified gross body.

I am the enlightened Deity Heruka,
The nature of my purified white indestructible drop,
With my consort Vajravarahi,
The nature of my purified red indestructible drop.
I am surrounded by the Bodhisattva Deities, the
    Heroes and Heroines,
Who are the nature of my purified channels and
    drops.

Through enjoying great bliss and the emptiness of all
     phenomena I have pacified all ordinary appearances
     and conceptions,
And thus I have accomplished the real meaning of
     human life.

Having generated myself as Heruka with consort,
I meditate briefly on my body as hollow and empty
     like space.
Within this body is my central channel possessing four
     characteristics.
Inside my central channel in the centre of the eight
     petals of the heart channel wheel
Is the union of my white and red indestructible drop,
     the size of a small pea,
Which is very clear and radiates five-coloured lights.
Inside this is my indestructible wind in the aspect of a
     letter HUM,
Which is actual Glorious Heruka.
My mind enters into the HUM and mixes with it like
     water mixing with water.
I hold this HUM, which is my indestructible wind
     and Heruka, with mindfulness and meditate on it
     single-pointedly.

Through stabilizing this meditation the movement of
     my inner winds of conceptions will cease.
Thus, I will perceive a fully qualified clear light.
Through completing the practice of this clear light
I will attain the actual Union of Great Keajra, the state
     of enlightenment.

This is the great kindness of Guru Heruka;
May I become just like you.

Avalokiteshvara

Essential Insights into the Avalokiteshvara Sadhana: *Prayers and Requests to the Buddha of Compassion*

Who is Avalokiteshvara? Avalokiteshvara is an enlight-ened being who is the manifestation of the compassion of all Buddhas; the compassion of all Buddhas appears as Avalokiteshvara. He is the synthesis of all Buddhas. In this context, sadhana refers to the ritual prayer for the attainment of Avalokiteshvara, the Buddha of Compassion. The actual sadhana can be found in Appendix III.

The benefits of engaging in the practice of this sadhana are immeasurable. Through sincerely practising the instructions presented in this sadhana we can first solve our own daily problems by controlling our desire, anger and ignorance, and then with this ability we can lead people throughout the world to the correct spiritual path through which they can find the real meaning of human life.

The main practice of this sadhana is training in purify-ing and transforming the six classes of living being, which is a very blessed instruction that comes from the *Ganden*

Emanation Scripture. The six classes of living being are: gods, demi-gods and human beings, the three higher classes of living being; and animals, hungry ghosts and hell beings, the three lower classes of living being. There are seven stages to practising this sadhana.

THE FIRST STAGE: GOING FOR REFUGE AND GENERATING BODHICHITTA

GOING FOR REFUGE

In this context, going for refuge refers to seeking refuge in Buddha, Dharma and Sangha. This means that we apply effort to receiving Buddha's blessings, to practising Dharma purely and to receiving help from pure spiritual practitioners, known as 'Sangha'. If we are unable to do this practice we will not enter Buddhism, and if we do not enter Buddhism we will have no opportunity to attain permanent liberation from suffering or the supreme happiness of enlightenment. We will have then lost the real meaning of human life. Understanding this, in front of our Spiritual Guide, or an image of Buddha regarding it as a living Buddha, we make a promise to go for refuge to Buddha, Dharma and Sangha throughout this life and in life after life. This promise is the refuge vow. We can take this refuge vow through reciting the following refuge prayer three times, while concentrating on its meaning:

I and all sentient beings until we achieve enlightenment
Go for refuge to Buddha, Dharma and Sangha.

A detailed explanation of going for refuge can be found in Part Two of this book in the section *Meditation on Going for Refuge*.

GENERATING BODHICHITTA

'Bodhi' means enlightenment and 'chitta' means mind. Bodhichitta is a mind that spontaneously wishes to attain enlightenment to benefit each and every living being every day. We can generate this supreme good heart, bodhichitta, through reciting the following prayer three times while concentrating on its meaning:

Through the virtues I collect by giving and other perfections
May I become a Buddha for the benefit of all.

A detailed explanation of bodhichitta can be found in Part Two of this book in the section *Meditation on the Supreme Good Heart, Bodhichitta*.

THE SECOND STAGE:
VISUALIZING AVALOKITESHVARA

On the basis of this visualization we can begin, make progress in and complete our training in purifying and transforming the six classes of living being. To make a special connection with the six classes of living being we imagine that we are surrounded by the six classes of living being, all in the aspect of human beings. This will make our actions of benefiting the six classes of living being effective.

How do we visualize Avalokiteshvara? We contemplate again and again the meaning of the words from the sadhana, from 'I and all living beings as extensive as space' up to 'He is the synthesis of all objects of refuge.' Through this we will perceive a general image of Avalokiteshvara residing on our own crown and on the crowns of all those surrounding us, the six classes of living being. We should be satisfied with this rough general image. Then from our heart we strongly think, 'How wonderful if I myself were to become the Buddha of Compassion. May I become the Buddha of Compassion so that I can benefit each and every living being every day through my blessings and through my countless emanations.' With this supreme good heart we engage in the practice of the seven limbs.

THE THIRD STAGE:
THE PRACTICE OF THE SEVEN LIMBS

The practice of the seven limbs are: prostration, offering, purification, rejoicing, requesting, making a special request and dedication. As mentioned above, training in purifying and transforming the six classes of living being is the main practice, which is like the main body. The seven limbs are like limbs that support the main body. Without its limbs, a body cannot function. Similarly, without sincerely practising the seven limbs, training in purifying and transforming the six classes of living being cannot function. Understanding this we should recognize that the practice of the seven limbs is our daily practice.

Every day we should continually practise prostration, offering, purification and so forth, without forgetting them.

The objects to whom we prostrate, make offerings, confess, rejoice, request, and make a special request are the enlightened beings, and we dedicate our merit towards our own and others' enlightenment. Because of this the practice of the seven limbs is a powerful method to continually grow our potential for attaining enlightenment, our Buddha nature; it causes our Buddha nature or seed to ripen very quickly so that we will attain enlightenment very quickly.

When we attain enlightenment through this special training we will have completed our training in purifying and transforming the six classes of living being. This is because the moment we attain enlightenment we will be able to purify all the impurities of the six classes of living being and to bestow pure and everlasting happiness on all of them. Detailed explanations about each of the seven limb practices can be found in the book *Joyful Path of Good Fortune*, and in sadhanas such as *Offering to the Spiritual Guide* and *The Hundreds of Deities of the Joyful Land* and their commentaries.

THE FOURTH STAGE: REQUESTING THE FIVE GREAT MEANINGS

First we make a mandala offering and then we engage in the actual request. We imagine that the entire universe transforms into the Pure Land of Buddha, and we offer this mandala to the Buddha of Compassion, Avalokiteshvara.

We then engage in *Requesting the five great meanings*, which are:

(1) Attaining permanent liberation from the cycle of impure life

(2) Developing and maintaining conventional bodhichitta and ultimate bodhichitta, the main paths to enlightenment

(3) Purifying non-virtuous actions and delusions completely

(4) Attaining the Pure Land of Buddha

(5) Attaining enlightenment

These are the general great meanings, and completing our training in purifying and transforming the six classes of living being is a particular great meaning. From our heart we strongly request Avalokiteshvara who is inseparable from our Spiritual Guide to bless our mental continuum so that we can complete this training. While concentrating on this meaning, we mentally repeat many times the following request prayer:

O Guru Avalokiteshvara, Buddha of Compassion,
Please bless my mental continuum quickly,
So that I will quickly complete
The training in purifying and transforming the six
classes of living being.

THE FIFTH STAGE: THE ACTUAL TRAINING IN PURIFYING AND TRANSFORMING THE SIX CLASSES OF LIVING BEING

This has two parts:

1 Training in meditation
2 Training in subsequent practice

TRAINING IN MEDITATION

We imagine and think,

Due to my single-pointed request to Guru Avalokiteshvara residing on my crown, five coloured rays of light, the nature of the omniscient wisdom of Avalokiteshvara, radiate from his body and dissolve into the entire world and all living beings, the six classes of living being. All the impurities of the entire world and the living beings who inhabit it are purified. The entire world becomes the Pure Land of Buddha and all living beings, the six classes of living being, become enlightened beings.

We meditate on this belief single-pointedly for as long as possible. This belief is a correct belief because it is non-deceptive and gives us great meaning. In each session we can repeat this meditation many times with the above request prayer.

Through sincerely and continually practising this meditation we will develop and maintain a spontaneous belief that the entire world is purified and has become the Pure Land of Buddha, and that all living beings, the six classes of living being, are purified and have become enlightened beings.

Through continually maintaining this belief, our ordinary appearance and conception will continually reduce and finally will cease completely. At that time we will have become an actual enlightened being, and we will be able to benefit each and every living being every day through our blessings and our countless emanations. We will have accomplished the real meaning of our human life. How wonderful!

TRAINING IN SUBSEQUENT PRACTICE, ALSO CALLED 'THE THREE RECOGNITIONS'

We practise this as follows. Out of meditation we should recognize that whatever we see is not other than its emptiness, we should recognize that whatever we hear is not other than its emptiness, and we should recognize that whatever we remember is not other than its emptiness. These are the three recognitions.

In the *Heart Sutra* Buddha said that there is no form other than emptiness. The meaning of these words is as follows. Because the real nature of form is the emptiness of form, when we perceive form, in truth we perceive only the emptiness of form, but because of ignorance we cannot understand this. The emptiness of form is the mere absence of form we normally see. The way form really exists is in dependence on its mere name. If we are satisfied with its mere name, form really exists; beyond the mere name it does not exist. We should also apply this to sounds and to all phenomena.

From this explanation we can clearly understand the meaning of the three recognitions. If, with clear understanding, we continually practise the three recognitions day and night without ever forgetting them, this is the quick method for completing our training in purifying and transforming the six classes of living being.

THE SIXTH STAGE: MANTRA RECITATION

The mantra we recite in this sadhana is OM MANI PÄME HUM. Externally it is a collection of six syllables, but internally it is the omniscient wisdom of Avalokiteshvara, which protects living beings from ordinary appearance and conception, the root of all suffering. The six syllables of this mantra indicate that if we continually recite this mantra with strong faith throughout our life we will be able to purify and transform the six classes of living being, including ourself. Understanding this we should enjoy reciting this mantra.

The meaning of this mantra is: with OM we are calling Avalokiteshvara, MANI means the precious jewel of enlightenment, PÄME means liberation and HUM means please bestow. Together the meaning is: 'O Avalokiteshvara, please bestow the precious jewel of enlightenment to liberate all living beings.' Through the recitation of this mantra we train in the compassionate mind of bodhichitta.

To accomplish a close retreat of Avalokiteshvara we need to recite this mantra one million times in conjunction with the sadhana.

THE SEVENTH STAGE: DEDICATION

We practise this as follows. Understanding that unbearable suffering pervades the entire world, and with deep compassion for all living beings, from our heart we mentally repeat the following dedication prayer continually, again and again, every day. This will cause Avalokiteshvara, who is the synthesis of all Buddhas, to enter and abide at our heart so that we can quickly complete our training in purifying and transforming the six classes of living being.

DEDICATION PRAYER:

Through the virtues I have accumulated
By training in compassion and wisdom,
May all the impurities of the six classes of living
    being be purified,
And thus may they all transform into enlightened
    beings.

PART TWO

Training in Meditation

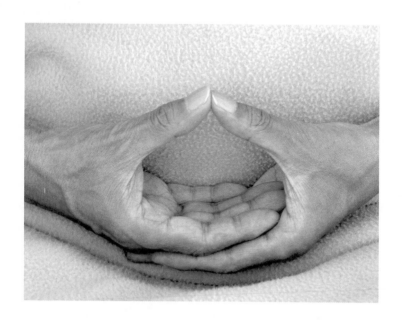

What is Meditation?

We should also put the advice from Je Tsongkhapa's heart, *The Three Principal Aspects of the Path to Enlightenment*, into practice by training in meditation on the stages of the path to enlightenment. This will now be explained.

In general, the definition of meditation is a mind that is single-pointedly focused on a virtuous object and whose function is to make the mind peaceful and calm.

We want to be happy all the time, even during sleep. How can we do this? We can do this through training in meditation because meditation makes our mind peaceful, and when our mind is peaceful we are happy all the time, even if our external conditions are poor. On the other hand, when our mind is not peaceful we are not happy, even if our external conditions are excellent. We can understand this through our own experience. Since the actual method to make our mind peaceful is training in meditation, we should apply effort to this training. Whenever we meditate, we are performing an action or karma that causes us to experience peace of mind in the future. From this we can understand the importance of training in meditation.

The difference between concentration and meditation is that concentration is necessarily a mental factor but meditation can be either a mental factor or a primary mind. We can understand the meaning of primary mind and mental factor from the book *How to Understand the Mind*. The object of concentration can be anything, but the object of meditation is necessarily a virtuous object. Whether an object is virtuous or non-virtuous depends on our position. For example, when our enemy harms us and we practise patience, our enemy is our virtuous object, the object of our patience, but if instead we get angry with him he is our non-virtuous object, the object of our anger. So it is our choice whether someone or something is our virtuous object or non-virtuous object. We should learn to use all living beings as our virtuous objects, the objects of our compassion and patience, and all phenomena as the objects of our training in emptiness. There is no greater Dharma practice than this.

There is a threefold division of meditation:

1 Meditation of a person of initial scope
2 Meditation of a person of middling scope
3 Meditation of a person of great scope

Meditation of a
Person of Initial Scope

There are five meditations of a person of initial scope:

1 Meditation on the preciousness of our human life
2 Meditation on death
3 Meditation on the danger of lower rebirth
4 Meditation on going for refuge
5 Meditation on karma

MEDITATION ON THE PRECIOUSNESS
OF OUR HUMAN LIFE

THE PURPOSE OF THIS MEDITATION

The purpose of this meditation is to encourage ourself to take the real meaning of our human life and not to waste it in meaningless activities. Our human life is very precious, but only if we use it to attain permanent liberation and the supreme happiness of enlightenment through practising Dharma purely and sincerely. We should encourage ourself to accomplish the real meaning of our human life. What is the real meaning of human life?

Many people believe that material development is the real meaning of human life, but we can see that no matter how much material development there is in the world it never reduces human suffering and problems. Instead, it often causes suffering and problems to increase; therefore it is not the real meaning of human life. We should know that at present we have reached the human world for just a brief moment from our former lives, and we have the opportunity to attain the supreme happiness of enlightenment through practising Dharma. This is our extraordinary good fortune. When we attain enlightenment we will have fulfilled our own wishes, and we can fulfil the wishes of all other living beings; we will have liberated ourself permanently from the sufferings of this life and countless future lives, and we can directly benefit each and every living being every day. The attainment of enlightenment is therefore the real meaning of human life.

As mentioned in Part One, enlightenment is the inner light of wisdom that is permanently free from all mistaken appearance, and whose function is to bestow mental peace on each and every living being every day. Right now we have obtained a human rebirth and have the opportunity to attain enlightenment through Dharma practice, so if we waste this precious opportunity in meaningless activities there is no greater loss and no greater foolishness. This is because in the future such a precious opportunity will be extremely hard to find. In one Sutra Buddha illustrates this by giving the following analogy. He asks his disciples, 'Suppose there existed a vast and deep ocean the size of this world, and on its surface there floated a golden yoke, and at the bottom of the ocean there lived a blind turtle who surfaced only once in every one hundred thousand years. How often would that turtle raise its head through the middle of the yoke?' His disciple, Ananda, answers that, indeed, it would be extremely rare.

In this context, the vast and deep ocean refers to samsara – the cycle of impure life that we have experienced since beginningless time, continually in life after life without end – the golden yoke refers to Buddhadharma, and the blind turtle refers to us. Although we are not physically a turtle, mentally we are not much different; and although our physical eyes may not be blind, our wisdom eyes are. For most of our countless previous lives we have remained at the bottom of the ocean of samsara, in the three lower realms – the animal, hungry ghost and hell realms – surfacing only once in every one hundred thousand years or so as a human being. Even when we briefly reach the upper realm of samsara's ocean as a human being, it is extremely rare to meet the golden yoke of Buddhadharma: the ocean of samsara is extremely vast, the golden yoke of Buddhadharma does not remain in one place but moves from place to place, and our wisdom eyes are always blind. For these reasons, Buddha says that in the future, even if we obtain a human rebirth, it will be extremely rare to meet Buddhadharma again; meeting Kadam Dharma is even rarer than this. We can see that the great majority of human beings in the world, even though they have briefly reached the upper realm of samsara as human beings, have not met Buddhadharma. This is because their wisdom eyes have not opened.

What does 'meeting Buddhadharma' mean? It means entering into Buddhism by sincerely seeking refuge in Buddha, Dharma and Sangha, and thus having the opportunity to enter and make progress on the path to enlightenment. If we do not meet Buddhadharma we have no opportunity to do this, and therefore we have no opportunity to accomplish the pure and everlasting happiness of enlightenment, the real meaning of human life.

THE OBJECT OF THIS MEDITATION

The object of this meditation, or the object on which we focus single-pointedly, is our determination to practise Dharma purely and sincerely. We should learn to develop this determination through contemplating the above explanation of the purpose of this meditation. When, through this contemplation, a firm determination to practise Dharma purely and sincerely develops in our heart, we have found the object of this meditation.

THE ACTUAL MEDITATION

We should think:

At present I have briefly reached the human world and have the opportunity to attain permanent liberation from suffering and the supreme happiness of enlightenment through putting Dharma into practice. If I waste this precious opportunity in meaningless activities there is no greater loss and no greater foolishness.

Thinking in this way we make the strong determination to practise Dharma, Buddha's teachings, of the stages of the path to enlightenment sincerely and purely, while we have the opportunity. We hold this determination in our heart without forgetting it and remain on it single-pointedly for as long as possible. Through continually training in this meditation we will develop a spontaneous wish to practise Dharma, the stages of the path, purely and sincerely. This wish is the realization of this meditation.

During the meditation break we should put our determination into practice.

MEDITATION ON DEATH

THE PURPOSE OF THIS MEDITATION

The purpose of this meditation is to prevent the laziness of attachment, the main obstacle to Dharma practice. Because our desire for worldly enjoyment is so strong, we have little or no interest in Dharma practice. From a spiritual point of view, this lack of interest in Dharma practice is a type of laziness called 'laziness of attachment'. For as long as we have this laziness, the door to liberation will be closed to us, and consequently we will continue to experience misery and suffering in this life and in countless future lives. The way to overcome this laziness, the main obstacle to our Dharma practice, is to meditate on death.

We need to contemplate and meditate on our death again and again until we gain a deep realization of death. Although on an intellectual level we all know that eventually we are going to die, our awareness of death remains superficial. Since our intellectual knowledge of death does not touch our hearts, each and every day we continue to think 'I will not die today, I will not die today.' Even on the day of our death, we are still thinking about what we will do tomorrow or next week. This mind that thinks every day 'I will not die today' is deceptive – it leads us in the wrong direction and causes our human life to become empty. On the other hand, through meditating on death we will gradually replace the deceptive thought 'I will not die today' with the non-deceptive thought 'I may die today.' The mind that spontaneously thinks each and every day 'I may die today' is the realization of death. It is this realization that directly eliminates our laziness of attachment and opens the door to the spiritual path.

In general, we may die today or we may not die today – we do not know. However, if we think each day 'I may not die today', this thought will deceive us because it comes from our ignorance; whereas if instead we think each day 'I may die today', this thought will not deceive us because it comes from our wisdom. This beneficial thought will prevent our laziness of attachment, and will encourage us to prepare for the welfare of our countless future lives or to put great effort into entering the path to liberation and enlightenment. In this way, we will make our present human life meaningful. Until now we have wasted our countless former lives without any meaning; we have brought nothing with us from our former lives except delusions and suffering.

Our death is the permanent separation of our body and mind. We may experience many temporary separations of our body and mind, but these are not our death. For example, when those who have completed their training in the practice known as 'transference of consciousness' engage in meditation, their mind separates from their body. Their body remains where they are meditating, and their mind goes to a Pure Land and then returns to their body. At night, during dreams, our body remains in bed but our mind goes to various places of the dream world and then returns to our body. These separations of our body and mind are not our death because they are only temporary.

At death our mind separates from our body permanently. Our body remains at the place of this life but our mind goes to various places of our future lives, like a bird leaving one nest and flying to another. This clearly shows the existence of our countless future lives, and that the nature and function of our body and mind are very different. Our body is a visual form that possesses colour and shape, but, as explained in Part One, our mind is a formless continuum that always lacks colour and shape. The nature of our mind is empty like space, and its function is to perceive or understand objects. Through this we can understand that our brain is not our mind. The brain is simply a part of our body that, for example, can be photographed, whereas our mind cannot.

We may not be happy to hear about our death, but contemplating and meditating on death is very important for the effectiveness of our Dharma practice. This is because it prevents the main obstacle to our Dharma practice – the laziness of attachment to the things of this life – and it encourages us to practise Dharma purely right now. If we do this we will accomplish the real meaning of human life before our death.

THE OBJECT OF THIS MEDITATION

The object of this meditation is our thought 'I may die today, I may die today.' We should learn to develop this thought through contemplating the above explanation of the purpose of this meditation. When, through this contemplation, the thought 'I may die today, I may die today' develops in our heart, we have found the object of this meditation.

THE ACTUAL MEDITATION

We contemplate and think:

I will definitely die. There is no way to prevent my body from finally decaying. Day by day, moment by moment, my life is slipping away. I have no idea when I will die; the time of death is completely uncertain. Many young people die before their parents, some die the moment they are born – there is no certainty in this world. Furthermore, there are so many causes of untimely death. The lives of many strong and healthy people are destroyed by accidents. There is no guarantee that I will not die today.

Having repeatedly contemplated these points, we mentally repeat over and over again, 'I may die today, I may die today', and concentrate on this belief. We transform our mind into this belief 'I may die today' and remain on it single-pointedly for as long as possible. Through continually training in this meditation we will develop each and every day the spontaneous belief 'I may die today'. This belief is the realization of this meditation.

During the meditation break we think, 'Since I will soon have to depart from this world, there is no sense in my becoming attached to the things of this life. Instead, from now on I will devote my whole life to practising Dharma purely and sincerely.' We then maintain this determination day and night, without laziness.

We need to apply effort in our Dharma practice. Realizing that worldly pleasures are deceptive, and that they distract us from using our life in a meaningful way, we should abandon attachment to them. In this way, we can eliminate laziness, the main obstacle to pure Dharma practice.

MEDITATION ON THE DANGER OF LOWER REBIRTH

THE PURPOSE OF THIS MEDITATION

The purpose of this meditation is to encourage us to prepare protection from the dangers of lower rebirth. If we do not do this now, while we have a human life with its freedoms and endowments and we have the opportunity to do so, it will be too late once we have taken any of the three lower rebirths; and it will be extremely difficult to obtain such a precious human life again. A precious human life means a human rebirth in which we have the opportunity to attain permanent liberation from all suffering, known as 'nirvana'. It is said to be easier for human beings to attain enlightenment than it is for beings such as animals to attain a precious human rebirth. Understanding this will encourage us to abandon non-virtue, or negative actions, to practise virtue, or positive actions, and to seek refuge in Buddha, Dharma and Sangha (the supreme and pure spiritual practitioners); this is our actual protection.

Performing non-virtuous actions is the main cause of taking lower rebirth, whereas practising virtue and seeking refuge in Buddha, Dharma and Sangha are the main causes of taking a precious human rebirth. Heavy non-virtuous actions are the main cause of rebirth as a hell being, middling non-virtuous actions are the main cause of rebirth as a hungry ghost, and lesser non-virtuous actions are the main cause of rebirth as an animal. There are many examples given in Buddhist scriptures of how non-virtuous actions lead to rebirth in the three lower realms.

There was once a hunter whose wife came from a family of animal farmers. After he died he took rebirth as a cow belonging to his wife's family. A butcher then bought this cow, slaughtered it and sold the meat. The hunter was reborn seven times as a cow belonging to the same family, and in this way became food for other people.

In Tibet there is a lake called Yamdroktso, where many people from the nearby town used to spend their whole lives fishing. At one time a great Yogi with clairvoyance visited the town and said, 'I see the people of this town and the fish in this lake are continually switching their positions.' What he meant was that the people of the town who enjoyed fishing were reborn as the fish, the food of other people, and the fish in the lake were reborn as the people who enjoyed fishing. In this way, changing their physical aspect, they were continually killing and eating each other. This cycle of misery continued from generation to generation.

THE OBJECT OF THIS MEDITATION

The object of this meditation is our feeling of fear of taking rebirth in the lower realms as an animal, a hungry ghost or a hell being. We should learn to develop this feeling of fear through contemplating the above explanation of the purpose of this meditation. When, through this contemplation, a feeling of fear of taking such a rebirth develops in our heart, we have found the object of this meditation.

In general fear is meaningless, but the fear generated here has great meaning. It arises from our wisdom and directly leads us to prepare the actual protection from taking lower rebirth, which is sincerely seeking refuge in Buddha, Dharma and Sangha, or in Guru Sumati Buddha Heruka. As the result of this, our next rebirth will be a precious human rebirth, which will give us the opportunity to continually make progress in our practice of Dharma, both Sutra and Tantra. Or our next rebirth will be in Keajra Pure Land through being led by Guru Sumati Buddha Heruka. If we do not generate this fear now we will never prepare these protections.

THE ACTUAL MEDITATION

We contemplate as follows:

When the oil of an oil lamp is exhausted, the flame goes out because the flame is produced from the oil; but when our body dies our consciousness is not extinguished, because consciousness is not produced from the body. When we die our mind has to leave this present body, which is just a temporary abode, and find another body, rather like a bird leaving one nest to fly to another. Our mind has no freedom to remain and no choice about where to go. We are blown to the place of our next rebirth by the winds of our actions or karma (our good fortune or misfortune). If the karma that ripens at our death time is negative, we will definitely take a lower rebirth. Heavy negative karma causes rebirth in hell, middling negative karma causes rebirth as a hungry ghost, and lesser negative karma causes rebirth as an animal.

It is very easy to commit heavy negative karma. For example, simply by swatting a mosquito out of anger we create the cause to be reborn in hell. Throughout this and all our countless previous lives we have committed many heavy negative actions. Unless we have already purified these actions by practising sincere confession, their potentials remain in our mental continuum, and any one of these negative potentials could ripen when we die. Bearing this in mind, we should ask ourself, 'If I die today, where will I be tomorrow? It is quite possible that I will find myself in the animal realm, among the hungry ghosts, or in hell. If someone were to call me a stupid cow today, I would find it difficult to bear, but what will I do if I actually become a cow, a pig or a fish – the food of human beings?'

Having repeatedly contemplated these points we generate a strong fear of taking rebirth in the lower realms. We then hold this without forgetting it; our mind should remain on this feeling of fear single-pointedly for as long as possible. Through continually training in this meditation we will develop a spontaneous feeling of fear of taking lower rebirth. This feeling of fear is the realization of this meditation.

During the meditation break we try never to forget our feeling of fear of taking rebirth in the lower realms.

MEDITATION ON GOING FOR REFUGE

THE PURPOSE OF THIS MEDITATION

The purpose of this meditation is to protect ourself permanently from taking lower rebirth. In this context, 'going for refuge' means seeking refuge in Buddha, Dharma and Sangha. At present, because we are human, we are free from rebirth as an animal, hungry ghost or hell being, but this is only temporary. We are like a prisoner who gets permission to stay at home for a week, but then has to return to prison. We need permanent liberation from the sufferings of this life and countless future lives. This depends on entering, making progress on and completing the Buddhist path to liberation, which in turn depends on entering Buddhism.

We enter Buddhism through the practice of going for refuge. For our practice of refuge to be qualified, while visualizing Buddha in front of us we should verbally or mentally make the promise to seek refuge in Buddha, Dharma and Sangha throughout our life. This promise is our refuge vow, and is the gateway through which we enter Buddhism. For as long as we keep this promise we are inside Buddhism, but if we break this promise we are outside. By entering and remaining inside Buddhism we have the opportunity to begin, make progress on and complete the Buddhist path to liberation and enlightenment.

We should never give up our promise to seek refuge in Buddha, Dharma and Sangha throughout our life. Going for refuge to Buddha, Dharma and Sangha means that we apply effort to receiving Buddha's blessings, to putting Dharma into practice and to receiving help from Sangha. These are the three principal commitments of the refuge vow. Through maintaining and sincerely practising these three principal commitments of refuge we can fulfil our final goal.

The main reason why we need to make the determination and promise to seek refuge in Buddha, Dharma and Sangha throughout our life is that we need to attain permanent liberation from suffering. At present we may be free from physical suffering and mental pain, but as mentioned earlier this freedom is only temporary. Later in this life and in our countless future lives we will have to experience unbearable physical suffering and mental pain continually, in life after life without end.

When our life is in danger or we are threatened by someone, we usually seek refuge in the police. Of course, sometimes the police can protect us from a particular danger, but they cannot give us permanent liberation from death. When we are seriously ill we seek refuge in doctors. Sometimes doctors can cure a particular illness, but no doctor can give us permanent liberation from sickness. What we really need is permanent liberation from all sufferings, and as human beings we can achieve this only by seeking refuge in Buddha, Dharma and Sangha.

Buddhas are 'awakened', which means that they have awakened from the sleep of ignorance and are free from the dreams of samsara, the cycle of impure life. They are completely pure beings who are permanently free from all delusions and mistaken appearance. Buddha's function is to bestow mental peace on each and every living being every day by giving blessings. We know that we are happy when our mind is peaceful, and unhappy when it is not. It is therefore clear that our happiness depends on our having a peaceful mind and not on good external conditions. Even if our external conditions are poor, if we maintain a peaceful mind all the time we will always be happy. Through continually receiving Buddha's blessings we can maintain a peaceful mind all the time. Buddha is therefore the source of our happiness. Dharma is the actual protection through which we are permanently released from the sufferings of sickness, ageing, death and rebirth; and Sangha are the supreme spiritual practitioners who guide us to correct spiritual paths. Through these three precious wishfulfilling jewels, Buddha, Dharma and Sangha – known as the 'Three Jewels' – we can fulfil our own wishes as well as the wishes of all living beings.

Every day from the depths of our heart we should recite requesting prayers to the enlightened Buddhas, while maintaining deep faith in them. This is a simple method for us to receive the Buddhas' blessings continually. We should also join group prayers, known as 'pujas', organized at Buddhist Temples or Prayer Halls, which are powerful methods to receive the Buddhas' blessings and protection.

THE OBJECT OF THIS MEDITATION

The object of this meditation is our determination and promise to apply effort to accomplish the following three things: receiving Buddha's blessings, putting Dharma into practice and receiving help from Sangha, the pure spiritual practitioners including our Spiritual Teachers. We should learn to develop this determination and promise through contemplating the above explanation of the purpose of this meditation. When, through this contemplation, a firm determination to apply effort to accomplish these three things develops in our heart, we have found the object of this meditation.

THE ACTUAL MEDITATION

We should think:

I want to protect and liberate myself permanently from the sufferings of this life and countless future lives. I can accomplish this only by receiving Buddha's blessings, putting Dharma into practice and receiving help from Sangha – the supreme spiritual practitioners.

Thinking deeply in this way, we first make the strong determination and then the mental promise to apply effort to accomplish the three things mentioned above. We hold this determination and promise without forgetting, and we remain on this determination and promise single-pointedly for as long as possible. Through continually training in this meditation we will develop the spontaneous wish to apply effort to receiving Buddha's blessings, putting Dharma into practice and receiving help from Sangha. This wish is the realization of this meditation.

During the meditation break we should always apply effort to receiving Buddha's blessings, putting Dharma into practice and receiving help from Sangha, the pure spiritual practitioners including our Spiritual Teacher. This is how we go for refuge to Buddha, Dharma and Sangha. Through this we will accomplish our aim – permanent liberation from all the sufferings of this life and countless future lives, the real meaning of our human life.

To maintain our promise to go for refuge to Buddha, Dharma and Sangha throughout our life, and so that we and all living beings may receive Buddha's blessings and protection, we recite the following refuge prayer every day with strong faith:

I and all sentient beings, until we achieve enlightenment,
Go for refuge to Buddha, Dharma and Sangha.

MEDITATION ON KARMA

THE PURPOSE OF THIS MEDITATION

The purpose of this meditation is to prevent future suffering and to build the basic foundation for the path to liberation and enlightenment. Generally, karma means 'action'. From non-virtuous actions comes suffering and from virtuous actions comes happiness: if we believe this, we believe in karma. Buddha gave extensive teachings that prove the truth of this statement and, as mentioned in Part One, many different examples that show the special connection between the actions of our former lives and our experiences of this life, some of which are explained in the book *Joyful Path of Good Fortune*.

Non-virtuous actions mean actions that are the opposite of virtue. Speaking generally, virtue means good fortune, which brings good results; and non-virtue means misfortune, which brings bad results. In our previous lives we performed various kinds of non-virtuous actions that caused others suffering. As a result of these non-virtuous actions, various kinds of miserable conditions and situations arise and we experience endless human suffering and problems. This is the same for all other living beings.

We should judge whether or not we believe that the main cause of suffering is our non-virtuous actions and the main cause of happiness is our virtuous actions. If we do not believe this we will never apply effort to accumulating virtuous actions, or merit, and we will never purify our non-virtuous actions, and because of this we will experience suffering and difficulties continually, in life after life without end.

Every action we perform leaves an imprint on our very subtle mind, and each imprint eventually gives rise to its own effect. Our mind is like a field, and performing actions is like sowing seeds in that field. Virtuous actions sow seeds of future happiness and non-virtuous actions sow seeds of future suffering. These seeds remain dormant in our mind until the conditions for them to ripen occur, and then they produce their effect. In some cases, this can happen many lifetimes after the original action was performed.

The seeds that ripen when we die are very important because they determine what kind of rebirth we will take in our next life. Which particular seed ripens at death depends on the state of mind in which we die. If we die with a peaceful mind, this will stimulate a virtuous seed and we will experience a fortunate rebirth. However, if we die with an unpeaceful mind, such as in a state of anger, this will stimulate a non-virtuous seed and we will experience an unfortunate rebirth. This is similar to the way in which nightmares are triggered by our being in an agitated state of mind just before falling asleep.

All inappropriate actions, such as killing, stealing, sexual misconduct, lying, divisive speech, hurtful speech, idle chatter, covetousness, malice and holding wrong views, and many other actions that cause others suffering, such as torturing or beating them, are non-virtuous actions. When we abandon non-virtuous actions and apply effort to purifying our previous non-virtuous actions we are practising moral discipline. This will prevent us from experiencing future suffering and from taking a lower rebirth. Examples of virtuous actions are consideration for others, sense of shame, compassion, showing loving kindness to others, benefiting others and, in particular, training in all the meditations and other spiritual practices presented in this book.

Meditation is a virtuous mental action that is the main cause of experiencing mental peace in the future. Whenever we practise meditation, whether or not our meditation is clear, we are performing a virtuous mental action that is a cause of our future happiness and peace of mind. We are normally concerned mainly about bodily and verbal actions, but in reality mental actions are more important. Our bodily and verbal actions depend on our mental action – on our mentally making a decision.

Whenever we perform virtuous actions such as meditation or other spiritual practices we should have the following mental determination:

While riding the horse of virtuous actions
I will guide it into the path of liberation with the reins of
*   renunciation;*
And through urging this horse onward with the whip of
*   effort,*
I will quickly reach the Pure Land of liberation and
*   enlightenment.*

THE OBJECT OF THIS MEDITATION

The object of this meditation is our determination to abandon and to purify our non-virtuous actions, and to accumulate virtuous actions or merit. We should learn to develop this determination through contemplating the above explanation of the purpose of this meditation. When, through this contemplation, a firm determination to abandon non-virtuous actions and to accumulate virtuous actions develops in our heart, we have found the object of this meditation.

THE ACTUAL MEDITATION

We contemplate and think:

Since I myself never wish to suffer and always want to be happy, I must abandon and purify my non-virtuous actions and sincerely perform virtuous actions.

We hold this determination firmly and remain on it single-pointedly for as long as possible. Through continually training in this meditation we will develop a spontaneous wish to abandon and purify non-virtuous actions and to accumulate virtuous actions. This wish is the realization of this meditation.

During the meditation break we should put our determination into practice.

Through the mirror of Buddha's teachings, Dharma,
we can see our own faults and have the
opportunity to remove them.

Meditation of a
Person of Middling Scope

There are four meditations of a person of middling scope:

1. Meditation on renunciation
2. Meditation on our determination to recognize, reduce and abandon our self-grasping ignorance, the root of samsaric rebirth
3. Meditation on our determination to engage in the actual path to liberation, the three higher trainings
4. Meditation on our determination to attain true cessations

MEDITATION ON RENUNCIATION

THE PURPOSE OF THIS MEDITATION

The purpose of this meditation is to enter, make progress on and complete the path to liberation. To achieve this aim we need to consider what we should know, what we should abandon, what we should practise and what we should attain.

In *Sutra of the Four Noble Truths* Buddha says, 'You should know sufferings.' In saying this Buddha is advising us that we should know about the unbearable sufferings that we will experience in our countless future lives, and therefore develop renunciation, the determination to liberate ourself permanently from these sufferings.

In general, everyone who has physical or mental pain, even animals, understands their own suffering; but when Buddha says 'You should know sufferings' he means that we should know the sufferings of our future lives. Through knowing these, we will develop a strong wish to liberate ourself from them. This practical advice is important for everybody because, if we have the wish to liberate ourself from the sufferings of future lives, we will definitely use our present human life for the freedom and happiness of our countless future lives. There is no greater meaning than this.

If we do not have this wish, we will waste our precious human life only for the freedom and happiness of this one short life. This would be foolish because our intention and actions would be no different from the intention and actions of animals who are only concerned with this life alone. The great Yogi Milarepa once said to a hunter called Gonpo Dorje:

Your body is human but your mind is that of an animal. You, a human being, who possess an animal's mind, please listen to my song.

Normally we believe that solving the suffering and problems of our present life is most important, and we dedicate our whole life for this purpose. In reality, the duration of the suffering and problems of this life is very short; if we die tomorrow, they will end tomorrow. However, since the duration of the suffering and problems of future lives is endless, the freedom and happiness of our future lives are vastly more important than the freedom and happiness of this one short life. With the words 'You should know sufferings' Buddha encourages us to use our present human life to prepare for the freedom and happiness of our countless future lives. Those who do this are truly wise.

In future lives, when we are born as an animal, such as a cow or a fish, we will become the food of other living beings, and we will have to experience many other kinds of animal suffering. Animals have no freedom, and are used by human beings for food, work and enjoyment. They have no opportunity to improve themselves; even if they hear precious Dharma words it is as meaningless to them as hearing the wind blowing. When we are born as a hungry ghost we will not have even a tiny drop of water to drink; our only water will be our tears. We will have to experience the unbearable sufferings of thirst and hunger for many hundreds of years. When we are born as a hell being in the hot hells our body will become inseparable from fire, and others will be able to distinguish between our body and fire only by hearing our suffering cries. We will have to experience the unbearable torment of our body being burned for millions of years. Like all other phenomena, the hell realms do not exist inherently but exist as mere appearances to mind, like dreams.

When we are born as a desire realm god we experience great conflict and dissatisfaction. Even if we experience some superficial enjoyment, still our desires grow stronger, and we have even more mental suffering than human beings. When we are born as a demi-god we are always jealous of the gods' glory and because of this we have great mental suffering. Our jealousy is like a thorn piercing our mind, causing us to experience both mental and physical suffering for long periods of time. When we are born as a human being we will have to experience various kinds of human suffering, including the sufferings of birth, sickness, ageing and death.

BIRTH

When our consciousness first enters the union of our father's sperm and our mother's ovum, our body is a very hot, watery substance like white yoghurt tinted red. In the first moments after conception we have no gross feelings, but as soon as these develop we begin to experience pain. Our body gradually becomes harder and harder, and as our limbs grow it feels as if our body is being stretched out on a rack. Inside our mother's womb it is hot and dark. Our home for nine months is this small, tightly compressed space full of unclean substances. It is like being squashed inside a small water tank full of filthy liquid with the lid tightly shut so that no air or light can come through.

While we are in our mother's womb we experience much pain and fear all on our own. We are extremely sensitive to everything our mother does. When she walks quickly it feels as if we are falling from a high mountain and we are terrified. If she has sexual intercourse it feels as if we are being crushed and suffocated between two huge weights and we panic. If our mother makes just a small jump it feels as if we are being dashed against the ground from a great height. If she drinks anything hot it feels like boiling water scalding our skin, and if she drinks anything cold it feels like an ice-cold shower in midwinter.

When we are emerging from our mother's womb it feels as if we are being forced through a narrow crevice between two hard rocks, and when we are newly born our body is so delicate that any kind of contact is painful. Even if someone holds us very tenderly, his or her hands feel like thorn bushes piercing our flesh, and the most delicate fabrics feel rough and abrasive. By comparison with the softness and smoothness of our mother's womb, every tactile sensation is harsh and painful. If someone picks us up it feels as if we are being swung over a huge precipice, and we feel frightened and insecure. We have forgotten all that we knew in our previous life; we bring only pain and confusion from our mother's womb. Whatever we hear is as meaningless as the sound of wind, and we cannot comprehend anything we perceive. In the first few weeks we are like someone who is blind, deaf and dumb, and suffering from profound amnesia. When we are hungry we cannot say 'I need food', and when we are in pain we cannot say 'This is hurting me.' The only signs we can make are hot tears and furious gestures. Our mother often has no idea what pains and discomforts we are experiencing. We are completely helpless and have to be taught everything – how to eat, how to sit, how to walk, how to talk.

Although we are most vulnerable in the first few weeks of our life, our pains do not cease as we grow up. We continue to experience various kinds of suffering throughout our life. Just as when we light a fire in a large house, the heat from the fire pervades the whole house and all the heat in the house comes from the fire, so when we take a samsaric rebirth, suffering pervades our whole life, and all the miseries we experience arise from this contaminated rebirth.

Our human rebirth, contaminated by the poisonous delusion of self-grasping, is the basis of our human suffering; without this basis, there are no human problems. The pains of birth gradually turn into the pains of sickness, ageing and death – they are one continuum.

SICKNESS

Our birth also gives rise to the suffering of sickness. Just as the wind and snow of winter take away the glory of green meadows, trees, forests and flowers, so sickness takes away the youthful splendour of our body, destroying its strength and the power of our senses. If we are usually fit and well, when we become sick we are suddenly unable to engage in all our normal physical activities. Even a champion boxer who is usually able to knock out all his opponents becomes completely helpless when sickness strikes. Sickness makes all our experiences of daily enjoyments disappear and causes us to experience unpleasant feelings day and night.

When we fall ill, we are like a bird that has been soaring in the sky and is suddenly shot down. When a bird is shot, it falls straight to the ground like a lump of lead, and all its glory and power are immediately destroyed. In a similar way, when we become ill we are suddenly incapacitated. If we are seriously ill we may become completely dependent on others and lose even the ability to control our bodily functions. This transformation is hard to bear, especially for those who pride themselves on their independence and physical well-being.

When we are ill, we feel frustrated as we cannot do our usual work or complete all the tasks we have set ourself. We easily become impatient with our illness and depressed about all the things we cannot do. We cannot enjoy the things that usually give us pleasure, such as sport, dancing, drinking, eating rich foods, or the company of our friends. All these limitations make us feel even more miserable; and, to add to our unhappiness, we have to endure all the physical pains the illness brings.

When we are sick, not only do we have to experience all the unwanted pains of the illness itself, but we also have to experience all sorts of other unwished for things. For example, we have to take whatever cure is prescribed, whether it be a foul-tasting medicine, a series of injections, a major operation, or abstinence from something we like very much. If we are to have an operation, we have to go to hospital and accept all the conditions there. We may have to eat food we do not like and stay in bed all day long with nothing to do, and we may feel anxiety about the operation. Our doctor may not explain to us exactly what the problem is and whether or not he or she expects us to survive.

If we learn that our sickness is incurable, and we have no spiritual experience, we will suffer anxiety, fear and regret. We may become depressed and give up hope, or we may become angry with our illness, feeling that it is an enemy that has maliciously deprived us of all joy.

AGEING

Our birth also gives rise to the pains of ageing. Ageing steals our beauty, our health, our good figure, our fine complexion, our vitality and our comfort. Ageing turns us into objects of contempt. It brings many unwanted pains and takes us swiftly to our death.

As we grow old we lose all the beauty of our youth, and our strong, healthy body becomes weak and burdened with illness. Our once firm and well-proportioned figure becomes bent and disfigured, and our muscles and flesh shrink so that our limbs become like thin sticks and our bones poke out. Our hair loses its colour and shine, and our complexion loses its lustre. Our face becomes wrinkled and our features grow distorted. Milarepa said:

How do old people get up? They get up as if they were heaving a stake out of the ground. How do old people walk about? Once they are on their feet they have to walk gingerly, like bird-catchers. How do old people sit down? They crash down like heavy luggage whose harness has snapped.

We can contemplate the following poem on the sufferings of growing old, written by the scholar Gungtang:

When we are old, our hair becomes white,
But not because we have washed it clean;
It is a sign we will soon encounter the Lord of Death.

We have wrinkles on our forehead,
But not because we have too much flesh;

It is a warning from the Lord of Death: 'You are about
    to die.'

Our teeth fall out,
But not to make room for new ones;
It is a sign we will soon lose the ability to eat human
    food.

Our faces are ugly and unpleasant,
But not because we are wearing masks;
It is a sign we have lost the mask of youth.

Our heads shake to and fro,
But not because we are in disagreement;
It is the Lord of Death striking our head with the stick
    he holds in his right hand.

We walk bent and gazing at the ground,
But not because we are searching for lost needles;
It is a sign we are searching for our lost beauty and
    memories.

We get up from the ground using all four limbs,
But not because we are imitating animals;
It is a sign our legs are too weak to support our body.

We sit down as if we had suddenly fallen,
But not because we are angry;
It is a sign our body has lost its strength.

Our body sways as we walk,
But not because we think we are important;
It is a sign our legs cannot carry our body.

Our hands shake,
But not because they are itching to steal;
It is a sign the Lord of Death's itchy fingers are stealing
    our possessions.

We eat very little,
But not because we are miserly;
It is a sign we cannot digest our food.

We wheeze frequently,
But not because we are whispering mantras to the sick;
It is a sign our breathing will soon disappear.

When we are young we can travel around the whole world, but when we are old we can hardly make it to our own front door. We become too weak to engage in many worldly activities, and our spiritual activities are often curtailed. For example, we have little physical strength to perform virtuous actions, and little mental energy to memorize, contemplate and meditate. We cannot attend teachings that are given in places that are hard to reach or uncomfortable to inhabit. We cannot help others in ways that require physical strength and good health. Deprivations such as these often make old people very sad.

When we grow old, we become like someone who is blind and deaf. We cannot see clearly, and we need stronger and stronger glasses until we can no longer read. We cannot hear clearly, and so it becomes more and more difficult to listen to music or to the television, or to hear what others are saying. Our memory fades. All activities, worldly and spiritual, become more difficult. If we practise meditation it becomes harder for us to gain realizations because our memory and concentration are too weak. We cannot apply ourself to study. Thus, if we have not learnt and trained in spiritual practices when we were younger, the only thing to do when we grow old is to develop regret and wait for the Lord of Death to come.

When we are old we cannot derive the same enjoyment from the things we used to enjoy, such as food, drink and sex. We are too weak to play games and we are often too exhausted even for entertainments. As our lifespan runs out we cannot join young people in their activities. When they travel about we have to stay behind. No one wants to take us with them when we are old, and no one wants to visit us. Even our own grandchildren do not want to stay with us for very long. Old people often think to themselves, 'How wonderful it would be if young people would stay with me. We could go out for walks and I could show them things'; but young people do not want to be included in their plans. As their life draws to an end, old people experience the sorrow of abandonment and loneliness. They have many special sorrows.

DEATH

Our birth also gives rise to the sufferings of death. If during our life we have worked hard to acquire possessions, and if we have become very attached to them, we will experience great suffering at the time of death, thinking 'Now I have to leave all my precious possessions behind.' Even now we find it difficult to lend one of our most treasured possessions to someone else, let alone to give it away. No wonder we become so miserable when we realize that in the hands of death we must abandon everything.

When we die we have to part from even our closest friends. We have to leave our partner, even though we may have been together for years and never spent a day apart. If we are very attached to our friends we will experience great misery at the time of death, but all we will be able to do is hold their hands. We will not be able to halt the process of death, even if they plead with us not to die. Usually when we are very attached to someone we feel jealous if he or she leaves us on our own and spends time with someone else, but when we die we will have to leave our friends with others forever. We will have to leave everyone, including our family and all the people who have helped us in this life.

When we die, this body that we have cherished and cared for in so many ways will have to be left behind. It will become mindless like a stone, and will be buried in the ground or cremated. If we do not have the inner protection of spiritual experience, at the time of death we will experience fear and distress, as well as physical pain.

When our consciousness departs from our body at death, all the potentials we have accumulated in our mind by performing virtuous and non-virtuous actions will go with it. Other than these we cannot take anything out of this world. All other things deceive us. Death ends all our activities – our conversation, our eating, our meeting with friends, our sleep. Everything draws to a close on the day of our death and we must leave all things behind, even the rings on our fingers. In Tibet beggars carry a stick to defend themselves against dogs. To understand the complete deprivation of death we should remember that at the time of death beggars have to leave even this old stick, the most meagre of human possessions. All over the world we can see that names carved on stone are the only possessions of the dead.

OTHER TYPES OF SUFFERING

We also have to experience the sufferings of separation, having to encounter what we do not like and not fulfilling our wishes – which include the sufferings of poverty, and of being harmed by humans and non-humans and by water, fire, wind and earth. Before the final separation at the time of death we often have to experience temporary separation from the people and things we like, which causes us mental pain. We may have to leave our country where all our friends and relatives live, or we may have to leave the job we like. We may lose our reputation. Many times in this life we have to experience the misery of departing from the people we like, or forsaking and losing the things we find pleasant and attractive; but when we die we have to part forever from all our companions and enjoyments, and from all the outer and inner conditions for our Dharma practice, of this life.

We often have to meet and live with people whom we do not like, or encounter situations that we find unpleasant. Sometimes we may find ourself in a very dangerous situation such as in a fire or a flood, or where there is violence such as in a riot or a battle. Our lives are full of less extreme situations that we find annoying. Sometimes we are prevented from doing the things we want to do. On a sunny day we may set off for the beach but find ourself stuck in a traffic jam. We continually experience interference from our inner demon of delusions, which disturbs our mind and our spiritual practices. There are countless conditions that frustrate our plans and prevent us from doing what we want. It is as if we are naked and living in a thorn bush – whenever we try to move, we are wounded by circumstances. People and things are like thorns piercing our flesh and no situation ever feels entirely comfortable. The more desires and plans we have, the more frustrations we experience. The more we want certain situations, the more we find ourself stuck in situations we do not want. Every desire seems to invite its own obstacle. Undesired situations befall us without our looking for them. In fact, the only things that come effortlessly are the things we do not want. No one wants to die, but death comes effortlessly. No one wants to be sick, but sickness comes effortlessly. Because we have taken rebirth without freedom or control, we have an impure body and inhabit an impure environment, and so undesirable things pour in on us. In samsara, this kind of experience is entirely natural.

We have countless desires, but no matter how much effort we make we never feel that we have satisfied them. Even when we get what we want, we do not get it in the way we want. We possess the object but we do not derive satisfaction from possessing it. For example, we may dream of becoming wealthy, but if we actually become wealthy our life is not the way we imagined it would be, and we do not feel that we have fulfilled our desire. This is because our desires do not decrease as our wealth increases. The more wealth we have, the more we desire. The wealth we seek is unfindable because we seek an amount that will satiate our desires, and no amount of wealth can do that. To make things worse, in obtaining the object of our desire we create new occasions for discontent. With every object we desire come other objects we do not want. For example, with wealth come taxes, insecurity and complicated financial affairs. These unwished for side effects prevent us from ever feeling fully satisfied. Similarly, we may dream of having a holiday in an exotic location, and we may actually go there on holiday, but the experience is never quite what we expect, and with our holiday come other things such as sunburn and great expense.

If we examine our desires we will see that they are excessive. We want all the best things in samsara – the best job, the best partner, the best reputation, the best house, the best car, the best holiday. Anything that is not the best leaves us with a feeling of disappointment – still searching for but not finding what we want. No worldly enjoyment, however, can give us the complete and perfect satisfaction we desire. Better things are always being produced. Everywhere, new advertisements announce that the very best thing has just arrived on the market, but a few days later another best thing arrives that is better than the best thing of a few days ago. There is no end of new things to captivate our desires.

Children at school can never satisfy their own or their parents' ambitions. Even if they come top of their class they feel they cannot be content unless they do the same the following year. If they go on to be successful in their jobs, their ambitions will be as strong as ever. There is no point at which they can rest, feeling that they are completely satisfied with what they have done.

We may think that at least people who lead a simple life in the country must be content, but if we look at their situation we will find that even farmers search for but do not find what they want. Their lives are full of problems and anxieties, and they do not enjoy real peace and satisfaction. Their livelihoods depend on many uncertain factors beyond their control, such as the weather. Farmers have no more freedom from discontent than businessmen who live and work in the city. Businessmen look smart and efficient as they set off to work each morning carrying their briefcases but, although they look so smooth on the outside, in their hearts they carry many dissatisfactions. They are still searching for but not finding what they want.

If we reflect on this situation we may decide that we can find what we are searching for by abandoning all our possessions. We can see, however, that even poor people are looking for but not finding what they seek, and many poor people have difficulty in finding even the most basic necessities of life; millions of people in the world experience the sufferings of extreme poverty.

We cannot avoid the suffering of dissatisfaction by frequently changing our situation. We may think that if we keep getting a new partner or a new job, or keep travelling about, we will eventually find what we want; but even if we were to travel to every place on the globe, and have a new lover in every town, we would still be seeking another place and another lover. In samsara there is no real fulfilment of our desires.

Whenever we see anyone in a high or low position, male or female, they differ only in appearance, dress, behaviour and status. In essence they are all equal – they all experience problems in their lives. Whenever we have a problem, it is easy to think that it is caused by our particular circumstances, and that if we were to change our circumstances our problem would disappear. We blame other people, our friends, our food, our government, our times, the weather, society, history and so forth. However, external circumstances such as these are not the main causes of our problems. We need to recognize that all the physical suffering and mental pain we experience are the consequences of our taking a rebirth that is contaminated by the inner poison of delusions. Human beings have to experience various kinds of human suffering because they have taken a contaminated human rebirth; animals have to experience animal suffering because they have taken a contaminated animal rebirth; and hungry ghosts and hell beings have to experience their own sufferings because they have taken contaminated rebirth as hungry ghosts and hell beings. Even gods are not free from suffering because they too have taken a contaminated rebirth. Just as a person trapped inside a raging fire develops intense fear, so we should develop intense fear of the unbearable sufferings of the endless cycle of impure life. This fear is real renunciation and arises from our wisdom.

THE OBJECT OF THIS MEDITATION

The object of this meditation is our determination to liberate ourself permanently from the sufferings of our countless future lives. This determination is renunciation. We should learn to develop this determination through contemplating the above explanation of the purpose of this meditation. When, through this contemplation, a firm determination to liberate ourself permanently from the sufferings of this life and of countless future lives develops in our heart, we have found the object of this meditation.

THE ACTUAL MEDITATION

From our heart we should think:

There is no benefit in denying the sufferings of future lives; when they actually descend upon me it will be too late to protect myself from them. Therefore I definitely need to prepare protection now, while I have this human life that gives me the opportunity to liberate myself permanently from the sufferings of my countless future lives. If I do not apply effort to accomplish this, but allow my human life to become empty of meaning, there is no greater deception and no greater foolishness. I must put effort now into liberating myself permanently from the sufferings of my countless future lives.

We hold this determination firmly and we remain on it single-pointedly for as long as possible. Through continually training in this meditation we will develop a spontaneous wish to liberate ourself permanently from the sufferings of our countless future lives. This wish is the realization of this meditation. The moment we develop this realization we enter the path to liberation. In this context, liberation refers to the supreme permanent peace of mind known as 'nirvana', which gives us pure and everlasting happiness.

During the meditation break we should put our determination into practice by making progress in our training on the actual path to liberation.

MEDITATION ON OUR DETERMINATION TO RECOGNIZE, REDUCE AND ABANDON OUR SELF-GRASPING IGNORANCE, THE ROOT OF SAMSARIC REBIRTH

THE PURPOSE OF THIS MEDITATION

The purpose of this meditation is to fulfil the aim of our renunciation. In *Sutra of the Four Noble Truths* Buddha says, 'You should abandon origins.' In saying this Buddha is advising us that if we wish to liberate ourself permanently from the sufferings of our countless future lives we should abandon origins. 'Origins' means our delusions, principally our delusion of self-grasping. Self-grasping is called an 'origin' because it is the source of all our suffering and problems, and is also known as the 'inner demon'. Delusions are wrong awarenesses whose function is to destroy mental peace, the source of happiness; they have no function other than to harm us. Delusions such as self-grasping abide at our heart and continually harm us day and night without rest by destroying our peace of mind. In samsara, the cycle of impure life, no one has the opportunity to experience real happiness because their mental peace, the source of happiness, is continually being destroyed by the inner demon of self-grasping.

Our self-grasping ignorance is a mind that mistakenly believes that our self, our body and all the other things we normally see actually exist. Because of this ignorance we develop attachment to the things we like and anger at the things we do not like. We then perform various kinds of non-virtuous action, and as a result of these actions we experience various kinds of suffering and problems in this life and in life after life.

Self-grasping ignorance is an inner poison that causes far greater harm than any outer poison. Because of being polluted by this inner poison, our mind sees everything in a mistaken way, and as a result we experience hallucination-like sufferings and problems. In reality, our self, our body and all the other things we normally see do not exist. Self-grasping can be likened to a poisonous tree, all other delusions to its branches, and all our suffering and problems to its fruit; it is the fundamental source of all our other delusions and of all our suffering and problems. Through this we can understand that if we abandon our self-grasping permanently, all our suffering and problems of this life and of countless future lives will cease permanently. The great Yogi Saraha said: 'If your mind is released permanently from self-grasping, there is no doubt that you will be released permanently from suffering.' To release our mind from self-grasping we need to understand that our I and mine we normally see do not exist.

THE OBJECT OF THIS MEDITATION

The object of this meditation is our determination to abandon our self-grasping ignorance. We should learn to develop this determination through contemplating the above explanation of the purpose of this meditation. When, through this contemplation, a firm determination to abandon our ignorance of self-grasping develops in our heart, we have found the object of this meditation.

THE ACTUAL MEDITATION

From our heart we should think:

Since I want to liberate myself permanently from all the sufferings of this life and countless future lives, I must apply great effort to recognizing, reducing and finally abandoning my ignorance of self-grasping completely.

We hold this determination firmly and we remain on it single-pointedly for as long as possible. Through continually training in this meditation we will develop a spontaneous wish to recognize, reduce and finally cease completely our ignorance of self-grasping, the root of all suffering. This wish is the realization of this meditation.

During the meditation break we should put our determination into practice.

MEDITATION ON OUR DETERMINATION TO ENGAGE IN THE ACTUAL PATH TO LIBERATION, THE THREE HIGHER TRAININGS

THE PURPOSE OF THIS MEDITATION

The purpose of this meditation is to encourage ourself to engage in the actual path to liberation, the three higher trainings. In *Sutra of the Four Noble Truths* Buddha says, 'You should practise the path.' In this context, 'path' does not mean an external path that leads from one place to another, but an inner path, a spiritual realization that leads us to the pure happiness of liberation and enlightenment.

The practice of the stages of the path to liberation can be condensed into the three higher trainings: training in higher moral discipline, training in higher concentration and training in higher wisdom. These trainings are called 'higher' because they are motivated by renunciation. They are therefore the actual path to liberation that we need to practise.

The nature of moral discipline is a virtuous determination to abandon inappropriate actions. When we practise moral discipline we abandon inappropriate actions, maintain pure behaviour and perform every action correctly with a virtuous motivation. Moral discipline is most important for everybody in order to prevent future problems for ourself and for others. It makes us pure because it makes our actions pure. We need to be clean and pure ourself; just having a clean body is not enough, since our body is not our self. Moral discipline is like a great earth that supports and nurtures the crops of spiritual realizations. Without practising moral discipline, it is very difficult to make progress in spiritual training. Training in higher moral discipline is learning to be deeply familiar with the practice of moral discipline, motivated by renunciation.

The second higher training is training in higher concentration. In this practice, the nature of concentration is a single-pointed virtuous mind. For as long as we remain with this mind we will experience mental peace, and thus we will be happy. When we practise concentration we prevent distractions and concentrate on virtuous objects. It is very important to train in concentration, as with distractions we cannot accomplish anything. Training in higher concentration is learning to be deeply familiar with the ability to stop distractions and concentrate on virtuous objects, with a motivation of renunciation. With regard to any Dharma practice, if our concentration is clear and strong it is very easy to make progress. Normally, distraction is the main obstacle to our Dharma practice. The practice of moral discipline prevents gross distractions, and concentration prevents subtle distractions; together they give rise to quick results in our Dharma practice.

The third higher training is training in higher wisdom. The nature of wisdom is a virtuous intelligent mind that functions to understand meaningful objects such as the existence of past and future lives, karma and emptiness. This book presents many different meditation practices. The objects of all these meditations are meaningful objects. Understanding these objects gives us great meaning in this life and in countless future lives. Many people are very intelligent in destroying their enemies, caring for their families, finding what they want and so forth, but this is not wisdom. Even animals have such intelligence. Worldly intelligence is deceptive, whereas wisdom will never deceive us. It is our inner Spiritual Guide who leads us to correct paths, and it is the divine eye through which we can see past and future lives, and the special connection between our actions in past lives and our experiences in this life, known as 'karma'. The subject of karma is very extensive and subtle, and we can understand it only through wisdom. Training in higher wisdom is learning to develop and increase our wisdom realizing emptiness through contemplating and meditating on emptiness with a motivation of renunciation. This wisdom is extremely profound. Its object, emptiness, is not nothingness but is the real nature of all phenomena. An essential explanation of emptiness is given in this book in the section *Training in Meditation on Emptiness*, and a detailed explanation of emptiness is given in the book *Modern Buddhism*, in the chapter on *Training in Ultimate Bodhichitta*.

At this point we should know that persons, phenomena, samsara, nirvana, suffering and happiness exist because they have a function. However, the persons, phenomena, samsara, nirvana, suffering and happiness we normally see or perceive do not exist because they are mistaken appearances and false objects that are not real objects of knowledge. From this we can understand that there is no contradiction between meditating on renunciation or compassion and meditating on selflessness, or emptiness.

The three higher trainings are the actual method to attain permanent liberation from the suffering of this life and countless future lives. This can be understood by the following analogy. When we cut down a tree using a saw, the saw alone cannot cut the tree without the use of our hands, which in turn depend on our body. Training in higher moral discipline is like our body, training in higher concentration is like our hands, and training in higher wisdom is like the saw. By using these three together, we can cut down the poisonous tree of our self-grasping ignorance, and automatically all other delusions – its branches – and all our suffering and problems – its fruits – will cease completely. Then we will have attained the permanent cessation of the suffering of this life and future lives – the supreme permanent peace of mind known as 'nirvana', or liberation. We will have solved all our human problems and accomplished the real meaning of our life.

THE OBJECT OF THIS MEDITATION

The object of this meditation is our determination to practise the three higher trainings. We should learn to develop this determination through contemplating the above explanation of the purpose of this meditation. When, through this contemplation, a firm determination to practise the three higher trainings develops in our heart, we have found the object of this meditation.

THE ACTUAL MEDITATION

From our heart we should think:

Since the three higher trainings are the actual method to attain permanent liberation from the suffering of this life and countless future lives, I must put great effort into practising them.

We hold this determination firmly and we remain on it single-pointedly for as long as possible. Through continually training in this meditation we will develop a spontaneous wish to practise the three higher trainings. This wish is the realization of this meditation.

During the meditation break we should put our determination into practice.

MEDITATION ON OUR DETERMINATION TO ATTAIN TRUE CESSATIONS

THE PURPOSE OF THIS MEDITATION

The purpose of this meditation is to prevent us from being satisfied with a merely temporary cessation of particular sufferings, which is deceptive. In *Sutra of the Four Noble Truths* Buddha says, 'You should attain cessations.' In this context, 'cessations' refers to true cessations, which means the permanent cessation of suffering and its root, self-grasping ignorance. In saying this, Buddha is advising us not to be satisfied with temporary liberation from particular sufferings, but that we should have the intention to accomplish the ultimate goal of human life, the supreme permanent peace of mind (nirvana), and the pure and everlasting happiness of enlightenment.

Every living being without exception has to experience the cycle of the sufferings of sickness, ageing, death and rebirth, in life after life, endlessly. Following Buddha's example, we should develop strong renunciation for this endless cycle. When he was living in the palace with his family, Buddha saw how his people were constantly experiencing these sufferings and he made the strong determination to attain enlightenment, great liberation, and to lead every living being to this state.

Buddha did not encourage us to abandon daily activities that provide necessary conditions for living, or that prevent poverty, environmental problems, particular diseases and so forth. However, no matter how successful we are in these activities, we will never achieve permanent cessation of such problems. We will still have to experience them in our countless future lives and, even in this life, although we work very hard to prevent these problems, the sufferings of poverty, environmental pollution and disease are increasing throughout the world. Furthermore, because of the power of modern technology there are now many great dangers developing in the world that have never been experienced before. Therefore, we should not be satisfied with merely temporary freedom from particular sufferings, but apply great effort to attaining permanent freedom while we have this opportunity.

We should remember the preciousness of our human life. Because of their previous deluded views denying the value of spiritual practice, those who have taken rebirth as animals, for example, have no opportunity to engage in spiritual practice, which alone gives rise to a meaningful life. Since it is impossible for them to listen to, understand, contemplate and meditate on spiritual instructions, their present animal rebirth itself is an obstacle. As mentioned earlier, only human beings are free from such obstacles and have all the necessary conditions for engaging in spiritual paths, which alone lead to everlasting peace and happiness. This combination of freedom and the possession of necessary conditions is the special characteristic that makes our human life so precious.

THE OBJECT OF THIS MEDITATION

The object of this meditation is our determination to attain permanent liberation from all the sufferings of this life and our countless future lives, known as 'nirvana'. We should learn to develop this determination through contemplating the above explanation of the purpose of this meditation. When, through this contemplation, a firm determination to attain permanent liberation from all the sufferings of this life and our countless future lives, the supreme inner peace of nirvana, develops in our heart we have found the object of this meditation.

THE ACTUAL MEDITATION

From our heart we should think:

I should not be satisfied with a merely temporary cessation of particular sufferings, which even animals can experience. I must attain the supreme inner peace of nirvana.

We should hold this determination firmly and remain on it single-pointedly for as long as possible. Through continually training in this meditation we will develop a spontaneous wish to attain permanent liberation, the supreme inner peace of nirvana. This wish is the realization of this meditation.

During the meditation break we should apply effort to put our determination into practice.

Like the sun dispelling clouds, we can develop the wisdom that can remove all delusions from our mind.

Meditation of a Person of Great Scope

There are six meditations of a person of great scope:

1. Meditation on cherishing all living beings
2. Meditation on universal compassion
3. Meditation on the supreme good heart, bodhichitta
4. Meditation on our determination and promise to sincerely practise the six perfections
5. Training in meditation on emptiness
6. Meditation on relying on our Spiritual Guide

MEDITATION ON CHERISHING ALL LIVING BEINGS

THE PURPOSE OF THIS MEDITATION

The purpose of this meditation is to develop universal compassion – compassion for all living beings. We should know that learning to cherish others is the best solution to our daily problems, and is the source of all our future happiness and good fortune. We believe that ourself we normally see is so important and its happiness and freedom are most important, and we neglect the happiness and freedom of others. This belief is ignorance, because ourself that we normally see does not actually exist. If we search for ourself that we normally see with wisdom, it will disappear. This proves that it does not exist at all. Therefore, our normal view believing that ourself is important but others are not is ignorance of self-cherishing. Because of this ignorance we have wasted countless former lives without any meaning. We brought nothing from our former lives except suffering and ignorance. This will be the same in our future lives. In truth, the happiness and freedom of others are more important than our own because we are only one person but others are countless. We must believe that the happiness and freedom of all other living beings are more important than our own.

THE OBJECT OF THIS MEDITATION

The object of this meditation is the belief that the happiness and freedom of all other living beings are more important than our own. We should learn to develop this belief through contemplating the above explanation of the purpose of this meditation. When, through this contemplation, a strong belief that the happiness and freedom of all other living beings are more important than our own develops in our heart, we have found the object of this meditation.

THE ACTUAL MEDITATION

From our heart we should think:

Just as all the Buddhas of the ten directions changed the object of their cherishing from themselves to all living beings, and as a result attained the supreme happiness of enlightenment, so must I do the same.

Thinking in this way we generate the strong belief that the happiness and freedom of all other living beings are more important than our own. We hold this view firmly and remain on it single-pointedly for as long as possible. Through continually training in this meditation we will develop a spontaneous belief that the happiness and freedom of all other living beings are more important than our own. This belief is the realization of this meditation.

During the meditation break we should never allow ourself to forget our belief that the happiness and freedom of all other living beings are more important than our own.

MEDITATION ON UNIVERSAL COMPASSION

THE PURPOSE OF THIS MEDITATION

The purpose of this meditation is to develop bodhichitta – the sincere wish to become an enlightened being to liberate all living beings. All the previous Buddhas were born from the mother of compassion for all living beings. We should follow their example and apply effort to generate compassion for all living beings without exception. The more our compassion for all living beings increases, the closer and closer we become to the attainment of enlightenment. This is because our compassion for all living beings makes our mind and our actions more and more pure, and when through this our mind and our actions become completely pure we become an enlightened being.

Universal compassion is a mind that sincerely wishes to permanently liberate all living beings from suffering. If, on the basis of cherishing all living beings, we contemplate the fact that they experience the cycle of physical suffering and mental pain in life after life without end, their inability to liberate themselves from suffering, their lack of freedom and how, by engaging in negative actions, they create the causes of future suffering, we will develop deep compassion for them. We need to empathize with them and feel their pain as keenly as we feel our own.

No one wants to suffer, yet out of ignorance living beings create suffering by performing non-virtuous actions. We should therefore feel equal compassion for all living beings without exception; there is no single living being who is not a suitable object of our compassion.

All living beings suffer because they take contaminated rebirths. Human beings have no choice but to experience immense human sufferings because they have taken human rebirth, which is contaminated by the inner poison of delusions. Similarly, animals have to experience animal suffering, and hungry ghosts and hell beings have to experience all the sufferings of their respective realms. If living beings were to experience all this suffering for just one single life, it would not be so bad, but the cycle of suffering continues life after life, endlessly.

To develop renunciation, we previously contemplated how in our countless future lives we will have to experience the unbearable sufferings of animals, hungry ghosts, hell beings, humans, demi-gods and gods. Now, at this point, to develop compassion for all living beings who are our mothers, we contemplate how in their countless future lives they will have to experience the unbearable sufferings of animals, hungry ghosts, hell beings, humans, demi-gods and gods.

THE OBJECT OF THIS MEDITATION

The object of this meditation is our determination to permanently liberate all living beings from suffering. We should learn to develop this determination through contemplating the above explanation of the purpose of this meditation. When, through this contemplation, a firm determination to permanently liberate all living beings from suffering develops in our heart, we have found the object of this meditation.

THE ACTUAL MEDITATION

From our heart we should think:

> *I cannot bear the suffering of these countless mother beings. Drowning in the vast and deep ocean of samsara, the cycle of contaminated rebirth, they have to experience unbearable*

physical suffering and mental pain in this life and in countless future lives. I must permanently liberate all these living beings from their suffering.

We hold this determination firmly and remain on it single-pointedly for as long as possible. Through continually training in this meditation we will develop the spontaneous wish to permanently liberate all living beings from suffering. This wish is the realization of this meditation.

During the meditation break we should never allow ourself to forget our determination to permanently liberate all living beings from suffering.

MEDITATION ON THE SUPREME GOOD HEART, BODHICHITTA

THE PURPOSE OF THIS MEDITATION

The purpose of this meditation is to engage in the Bodhisattva's path – the actual path to enlightenment. Bodhichitta is an inner vehicle that possesses six wheels, the six perfections. 'Bodhi' means enlightenment, and 'chitta' means mind. Bodhichitta is a mind that spontaneously wishes to attain enlightenment to benefit each and every living being every day. The moment we develop bodhichitta we become a Bodhisattva, a person who spontaneously wishes to attain enlightenment for the benefit of all living beings. Initially we will be a Bodhisattva on the path of accumulation. Then, by following the path to enlightenment with the vehicle of bodhichitta, we can progress from being a Bodhisattva on the path of accumulation to being a Bodhisattva on the path of preparation, a Bodhisattva on the path of seeing, and then a Bodhisattva on the path of meditation. From there we will reach the Path of No More Learning, which is the actual state of enlightenment. As already mentioned, enlightenment is the inner light of wisdom that is permanently free from all mistaken appearance, and whose function is to bestow mental peace on each and every living being every day. When we attain a Buddha's enlightenment we will be able to benefit each and every living being directly through bestowing blessings and through our countless emanations. In Sutra teachings, Buddha says:

> In this impure life of samsara
> No one experiences real happiness;
> The actions they perform
> Will always be the causes of suffering.

As mentioned in Part One, the happiness that we normally experience through having good conditions, such as a good reputation, a good position, a good job, good relationships, seeing attractive forms, hearing good news or beautiful music, eating, drinking and sex is not real happiness, but changing suffering – a reduction in our previous suffering. Out of ignorance, however, we believe that only these things bring happiness, and because of this we never wish to attain real happiness, the pure and everlasting happiness of liberation and enlightenment, even for our own benefit. We are always searching for happiness in this impure life of samsara, like the thief who searched for gold in Milarepa's empty cave and found nothing. The great Yogi Milarepa heard a thief rummaging around his cave one night and called out to him, 'How do you expect to find anything valuable here at night, when I cannot find anything valuable here during the day?'

When, through training, we develop the precious mind of enlightenment, bodhichitta, we spontaneously think:

How wonderful it would be if I and all living beings attained real happiness, the pure and everlasting happiness of enlightenment! May we attain this happiness. I myself will work for this aim.

We need to have this precious mind of bodhichitta in our heart. It is our inner Spiritual Guide, who leads us directly to the state of supreme happiness of enlightenment; and it is the real wishfulfilling jewel through which we can fulfil our own and others' wishes. There is no greater beneficial intention than this precious mind.

THE OBJECT OF THIS MEDITATION

The object of this meditation is our determination to attain enlightenment to benefit each and every living being every day. We should learn to develop this determination through contemplating the above explanation of the purpose of this meditation. When, through this contemplation, a firm deter-mination to attain enlightenment to benefit each and every living being every day develops in our heart, we have found the object of this meditation.

THE ACTUAL MEDITATION

From the depths of our heart we should think:

I am one single person but other living beings are countless, and they are all my kind mothers. These countless mother beings have to experience unbearable physical suffering and mental pain in this life and in their countless future lives. Compared with the suffering of these countless living beings, my own suffering is insignificant. I must liberate all living beings from suffering permanently, and for this purpose I must attain a Buddha's enlightenment.

We hold this determination firmly and remain on it single-pointedly for as long as possible. Through continually training in this meditation we will develop a spontaneous wish to attain enlightenment to benefit each and every living being every day. This wish is the realization of this meditation, and is the actual bodhichitta.

During the meditation break, to fulfil our bodhichitta wish we engage in training in the six perfections, the actual path to enlightenment, and we should emphasize the accumulation of merit and wisdom.

MEDITATION ON OUR DETERMINATION AND PROMISE TO SINCERELY PRACTISE THE SIX PERFECTIONS

THE PURPOSE OF THIS MEDITATION

The purpose of this meditation is to reach the state of enlightenment directly. The six perfections are the actual path to enlightenment, and they are also the path of bodhichitta and the Bodhisattva's path. Through following this path with the vehicle of bodhichitta we will definitely reach the state of enlightenment. Our bodhichitta wish is to attain enlightenment to benefit each and every living being directly. To fulfil this wish, in front of our Spiritual Guide or an image of Buddha regarded as the living Buddha, we should promise to engage in the Bodhisattva's path or training while reciting the following ritual prayer three times. This promise is the Bodhisattva's vow.

> *O Guru Buddha, please listen to me.*
> *Just as all the previous Sugatas, the Buddhas,*
> *Generated the mind of enlightenment, bodhichitta,*
> *And accomplished all the stages*
> *Of the Bodhisattva's training,*
> *So will I too, for the sake of all beings,*
> *Generate the mind of enlightenment*
> *And accomplish all the stages*
> *Of the Bodhisattva's training.*

When we take the Bodhisattva's vow we are taking the commitment to engage in the path to enlightenment, the Bodhisattva's training, which is the practice of the six perfections. Normally, when we start an ordinary job we commit ourself to fulfilling our employer's wishes; otherwise we will quickly lose our job. In the same way, having generated bodhichitta – the determination to attain enlightenment to benefit each and every living being directly – we need to commit ourself to engaging in the practice of the six perfections. If we do not make this commitment by taking the

Bodhisattva's vow, we will lose our opportunity to attain enlightenment. Through contemplating this we should encourage ourself to take the Bodhisattva's vow and sincerely practise the six perfections.

The six perfections are the practices of giving, moral discipline, patience, effort, concentration and wisdom, motivated by bodhichitta. We should recognize that the six perfections are our daily practice.

In the practice of giving we should practise: (1) giving material help to those in poverty, including giving food to animals; (2) giving practical help to those sick or physically weak; (3) giving protection by always trying to save others' lives, including those of insects; (4) giving love – learning to cherish all living beings by always believing that their happiness and freedom are important; and (5) giving Dharma – helping others to solve their problems of anger, attachment and ignorance by giving Dharma teachings or meaningful advice.

In the practice of moral discipline we should abandon any inappropriate actions including those that cause others suffering. We should especially abandon breaking our commitments of the Bodhisattva's vow. This is the basic foundation on which we can make progress on the Bodhisattva's path. By doing this our actions of body, speech and mind will be pure, so that we become a pure being.

In the practice of patience we should never allow ourself to become angry or discouraged, by temporarily accepting any difficulties or harm from others. When we practise patience we are wearing the supreme inner armour that directly protects us from physical sufferings, mental pain and other problems. Anger destroys our merit, or good fortune, so that we will continually experience many obstacles, and because of lacking good fortune it will be difficult to fulfil our wishes, especially our spiritual aims. There is no greater evil than anger. With the practice of patience we can accomplish any spiritual aim; there is no greater virtue than patience.

In the practice of effort we should rely on irreversible effort to accumulate the great collections of merit and wisdom, which are the main causes of attaining Buddha's Form Body (Rupakaya), and Truth Body (Dharmakaya); and especially we should emphasize contemplation and meditation on emptiness, the way things really are. By doing this we can easily make progress on the path to enlightenment. With effort we can accomplish our aim, whereas with laziness we cannot achieve anything.

In the practice of concentration, at this stage we should emphasize accomplishing the concentration of tranquil abiding observing emptiness. An explanation of this can be found in the book *Modern Buddhism* in the section *A Simple Training in Ultimate Bodhichitta*. When, through the power of this concentration, we experience a special wisdom called 'superior seeing' that realizes the emptiness of all phenomena very clearly, we will have progressed from being a Bodhisattva on the path of accumulation to being a Bodhisattva on the path of preparation.

In the practice of wisdom, at this stage we need to emphasize increasing the power of our wisdom of superior seeing by continually meditating on the emptiness of all phenomena with bodhichitta motivation. Through this, when our superior seeing transforms into the path of seeing, which is the direct realization of the emptiness of all phenomena, we will have progressed from being a Bodhisattva on the path of preparation to being a Bodhisattva on the path of seeing. The moment we attain the path of seeing we are a Superior Bodhisattva and no longer experience samsara's sufferings. Even if someone cuts our body piece by piece with a knife we have no pain because we have the direct realization of the way things really are.

Having completed the path of seeing, to make further progress we need to engage continually in the meditation on the emptiness of all phenomena with bodhichitta motivation. This meditation is called the 'path of meditation'. When we reach this stage we will have progressed from being a Bodhisattva on the path of seeing to being a Bodhisattva on the path of meditation.

Having completed the path of meditation, when our wisdom of the path of meditation transforms into an omniscient wisdom that is permanently free from all mistaken appearances, this omniscient wisdom is called the 'Path of No More Learning', which is actual enlightenment. When we reach this stage we will have progressed from being a Bodhisattva on the path of meditation to being an enlightened being, a Buddha. We will have completed the ultimate goal of living beings.

The Bodhisattva's initial training in accumulating merit or wisdom is the Bodhisattva's path of accumulation; the Bodhisattva's training in accumulating merit or wisdom that is a preparation for attaining the path of seeing is the Bodhisattva's path of preparation; the Bodhisattva's training that is the initial direct realization of emptiness is the

Bodhisattva's path of seeing; after completing the path of seeing, the Bodhisattva's training that meditates continually on emptiness is the Bodhisattva's path of meditation; and Buddha's omniscient wisdom that is attained through completing all the trainings of Sutra and Tantra is the Path of No More Learning, the state of enlightenment.

THE OBJECT OF THIS MEDITATION

The object in this meditation is our determination and promise to sincerely practise the six perfections. We should learn to develop this determination and promise through contemplating the above explanation of the purpose of this meditation. When, through this contemplation, a firm determination and promise to sincerely practise the six perfections develops in our heart, we have found the object of this meditation.

THE ACTUAL MEDITATION

From our heart we should think:

Just as all the previous Buddhas generated the precious mind of bodhichitta and accomplished all the stages of the Bodhisattva's path, so will I too for the sake of all living beings generate the precious mind of bodhichitta and accomplish all the stages of the Bodhisattva's path, the practice of the six perfections.

We hold this determination firmly and remain on it single-pointedly for as long as possible. Through continually engaging in this meditation we will develop a spontaneous wish to complete our training in the six perfections, the Bodhisattva's path. This wish is the realization of this meditation.

During the meditation break we should apply irreversible effort to training in the six perfections and to accumulating the collections of merit and wisdom. In this way we can make progress moment by moment towards the attainment of enlightenment.

TRAINING IN MEDITATION ON EMPTINESS

THE PURPOSE OF THIS MEDITATION

The purpose of this meditation is to permanently free our mind from all mistaken appearances, which are the main obstruction to the attainment of enlightenment. However, without understanding emptiness correctly there is no basis for this meditation. Therefore, with the following explanation we should strive to understand the meaning of emptiness. A simple explanation is as follows:

For example, we normally see our body within its parts – the hands, back and so forth – but neither the individual parts nor the collection of the parts are our body because they are the parts of our body and not the body itself. However, there is no 'our body' other than its parts. Through searching with wisdom for our body in this way, we realize that our body is unfindable. This is a valid reason to prove that our body we normally see does not exist at all.

Also, we normally see our self within our body and mind, but neither our body, nor our mind, nor the collection of our body and mind are our self, because these are our possessions and our self is the possessor; and possessor and possessions cannot be the same. However, there is no 'our self' other than our body and mind. Through searching with wisdom for our self in this way, we realize that our self is unfindable. This is a valid reason to prove that our self we normally see does not exist at all.

We should apply these reasons to all other phenomena, so that we will understand that all phenomena we normally see or perceive do not exist. In conclusion, we will understand that the real meaning of emptiness is the mere absence of all phenomena we normally see or perceive.

THE OBJECT OF THIS MEDITATION

The object of this meditation is the emptiness of all phenomena, the mere absence of all phenomena we normally see or perceive. We should learn to perceive clearly the mere absence of all phenomena we normally see or perceive through contemplating the above explanation of the purpose of this meditation. When, through this contemplation, a deep knowledge of the mere absence of all phenomena we normally see or perceive develops in our mind, we have found the object of this meditation.

THE ACTUAL MEDITATION

When a deep knowledge of the mere absence of all phenomena we normally see or perceive develops in our mind, we should hold this knowledge and remain on it single-pointedly without forgetting it. Through continually training in this meditation we will develop a deeper knowledge that functions to reduce or cease our self-grasping. This is the realization of this meditation.

During the meditation break we should learn to recognize that the things we normally see are like illusions; which means that although we see them they do not exist.

MEDITATION ON RELYING ON OUR SPIRITUAL GUIDE

THE PURPOSE OF THIS MEDITATION

The purpose of this meditation is to receive the powerful blessings of all Buddhas. We need to rely sincerely and purely on our Spiritual Guide. The reason for this is very simple. The ultimate goal of human life is to attain enlightenment, and this depends on continually receiving the special blessings of all Buddhas through our Spiritual Guide.

All Buddhas attained enlightenment with the sole intention of leading all living beings along the stages of the path to enlightenment through their emanations. Who is the emanation who is leading us along the stages of the path to enlightenment? It is clearly our present Spiritual Teacher, who is sincerely and correctly leading us along the paths of renunciation, bodhichitta and the correct view of emptiness by giving these teachings and showing a practical example for others to follow. Understanding this we should strongly believe that our Spiritual Guide is an emanation of Buddha, and develop and maintain deep faith in him or her.

THE OBJECT OF THIS MEDITATION

The object of this meditation is our deep faith in our Spiritual Guide. We should learn to develop this faith through contemplating the above explanation of the purpose of this meditation. When, through this contemplation, deep faith in our Spiritual Guide develops in our heart, we have found the object of this meditation.

THE ACTUAL MEDITATION

From the depths of our heart we should think:

It is clear that if I rely sincerely and purely on my Spiritual Guide I will receive the powerful blessings of all Buddhas through my Spiritual Guide, so that I can easily make progress in and complete my practice of both Sutra and Tantra. Through this I can fulfil my own and others' wishes.

In this way we generate deep faith in our Spiritual Guide and remain on it single-pointedly for as long as possible. Through continually training in this meditation we will develop the spontaneous faiths of admiring faith, believing faith and wishing faith, which is the realization of this meditation.

During the meditation break we should apply strong effort to sincerely practise our Spiritual Guide's teachings on renunciation, bodhichitta, correct view of emptiness, and the generation and completion stages of Tantra.

In summary, if we sincerely and continually practise the union of the stages of the paths of Sutra and Tantra we will quickly make progress from a lower state to higher and higher states until we become an enlightened being, a Buddha. This means that we will have permanently awakened from the sleep of ignorance, we will be able to see everything of the past, future and present directly and simultaneously, and we will become the source of happiness for all living beings. How wonderful!

Dorjechang Kelsang Gyatso Rinpoche

Dedication

Through the virtues I have accumulated by preparing this book may the Buddhadharma, the sole medicine for all suffering and the source of all happiness, be materially supported and honoured, and remain for a very long time. May there be permanent world peace, and may all living beings find a meaningful life.

Appendix I:
The Root Text:
The Three Principal Aspects of the Path to Enlightenment

by the Wisdom Buddha
Je Tsongkhapa

The Root Text:
The Three Principal Aspects of the Path to Enlightenment

Homage to the venerable Spiritual Guide.

I will explain to the best of my ability
The essential meaning of the teachings of all the Buddhas
    [renunciation],
The main path of the Bodhisattvas, who have compassion
    for all living beings [bodhichitta],
And the ultimate path of the fortunate ones who are
    seeking liberation [the correct view of emptiness].

You should not be attached to worldly enjoyments,
But strive to find the real meaning of human life
By listening to and practising the instructions given here,
Which all the previous Buddhas practised with delight.

Attachment to the fulfilment of your own wishes,
    uncontrolled desire,
Is the main cause of all your own problems and suffering,
And there is no method to abandon it without first
    developing renunciation.
Thus you should apply great effort to develop and
    maintain pure renunciation.

When, through daily training, you develop the
　　spontaneous thoughts:
'I may die today' and 'A precious human life is so rare',
And you meditate on the truth of karma and the
　　sufferings of the cycle of impure life, samsara,
Your attachment to worldly enjoyments will cease.

In this way, when uncontrolled desire for worldly
　　enjoyments
Does not arise even for a moment,
But a mind longing for liberation, nirvana, arises
　　throughout the day and the night,
At that time pure renunciation is generated.

However, if this renunciation is not maintained
By the compassionate mind of bodhichitta,
It will not be a cause of the unsurpassed happiness,
　　enlightenment;
Therefore, you must apply effort to generate the precious
　　mind of bodhichitta.

Swept along by the currents of the four powerful rivers
　　[birth, ageing, sickness and death],
Tightly bound by the chains of karma so hard to release,
Ensnared within the iron net of self-grasping,
Completely enveloped by the pitch-black darkness of
　　ignorance,

Taking rebirth after rebirth in boundless samsara,
And unceasingly tormented by the three sufferings
　　[painful feelings, changing suffering and pervasive
　　suffering] –

Through contemplating the state of your mothers, all
living beings, in conditions such as these,
Generate the supreme mind of bodhichitta.

But even though you may be acquainted with
renunciation and bodhichitta,
If you do not possess the wisdom realizing the way
things really are,
You will not be able to cut the root of samsara,
Therefore strive in the means for realizing dependent
relationship.

When you clearly see phenomena such as samsara and
nirvana, and cause and effect, as they exist,
And at the same time you see that all the phenomena
you normally see or perceive do not exist,
You have entered the path of the correct view of
emptiness,
Thus delighting all the Buddhas.

If you perceive and believe that the appearance,
phenomena,
And the empty, emptiness of phenomena,
Are dualistic,
You have not yet realized Buddha's intention.

Through just seeing that things exist
In dependence on their mere name,
If your self-grasping reduces or ceases,
At that time you have completed your understanding
of emptiness.

Moreover, if you negate the extreme of existence
By simply realizing that phenomena are just mere
appearance,
And if you negate the extreme of non-existence
By simply realizing that all the phenomena you
normally see or perceive do not exist,

And if you realize how, for example, the emptiness
of cause and effect
Is perceived as cause and effect,
Because there is no cause and effect other than
emptiness,
With these realizations you will not be harmed by
extreme view.

When, in this way, you have correctly realized the
essential points
Of the three principal aspects of the path,
Dear One, withdraw into solitary retreat, generate
and maintain strong effort
And quickly accomplish the final goal.

Appendix II:
Liberating Prayer

PRAISE TO BUDDHA SHAKYAMUNI

O Blessed One, Shakyamuni Buddha,
Precious treasury of compassion,
Bestower of supreme inner peace,

You, who love all beings without exception,
Are the source of happiness and goodness;
And you guide us to the liberating path.

Your body is a wishfulfilling jewel,
Your speech is supreme, purifying nectar,
And your mind is refuge for all living beings.

With folded hands I turn to you,
Supreme unchanging friend,
I request from the depths of my heart:

Please give me the light of your wisdom
To dispel the darkness of my mind
And to heal my mental continuum.

Please nourish me with your goodness,
That I in turn may nourish all beings
With an unceasing banquet of delight.

Through your compassionate intention,
Your blessings and virtuous deeds,
And my strong wish to rely upon you,

May all suffering quickly cease
And all happiness and joy be fulfilled;
And may holy Dharma flourish for evermore.

Colophon: This prayer was composed by Venerable Geshe
Kelsang Gyatso Rinpoche and is recited at the beginning
of teachings, meditations and prayers in Kadampa
Buddhist Centres throughout the world.

Appendix III:
Avalokiteshvara Sadhana

PRAYERS AND REQUESTS TO THE
BUDDHA OF COMPASSION

Avalokiteshvara

Introduction

Avalokiteshvara, or 'Chenrezig' in Tibetan, is an enlightened being who is a manifestation of all Buddhas' compassion. He is known as the 'Buddha of Compassion'. He usually appears as white in colour with four arms. His first two hands are pressed together at his heart, symbolizing his respect for his Spiritual Guide, Buddha Amitabha, who is on his crown. Even though Avalokiteshvara is an enlightened being, he still shows respect to his Spiritual Guide. His first two hands hold a jewel, which symbolizes his own enlightenment. This mudra is indicating, 'I attained jewel-like great enlightenment through receiving blessings from my Spiritual Guide Amitabha.'

His second left hand holds a white lotus flower. A lotus grows in the mud at the bottom of a lake, but its flowers bloom on the surface of the water, completely free from the stains of mud. By holding a lotus flower Avalokiteshvara is showing that, because he attained enlightenment, he is free from all obstacles and has a completely pure body, speech and mind. His second right hand holds a crystal mala, symbolizing that he can free all living beings from samsara and lead them to liberation.

If we rely sincerely upon Avalokiteshvara and recite his mantra with strong faith, temporarily we will improve our realizations of the stages of the path, especially our realization of great compassion, and ultimately we will attain supreme Buddhahood in Avalokiteshvara's Pure Land, the Pure Land of Bliss.

This sadhana is very blessed. The main body of the sadhana was composed by a great Tibetan Yogi called Drubchen Tangtong Gyalpo, who came from Ngam Ring Monastery in western Tibet. The prayer of seven limbs, offering the mandala, requesting the five great meanings, and the final dedication verse were later added from traditional sources.

Geshe Kelsang Gyatso
1978

Avalokiteshvara Sadhana

Going for refuge

I and all sentient beings, until we achieve enlightenment,
Go for refuge to Buddha, Dharma and Sangha.

(3x)

Generating bodhichitta

Through the virtues I collect by giving and other
    perfections,
May I become a Buddha for the benefit of all.

(3x)

Visualizing Arya Avalokiteshvara

I and all living beings as extensive as space
Have at our crowns a white lotus and a moon seat.
Upon these, from HRIH, arises Arya Avalokiteshvara.
He has a white, translucent body that radiates
    five-coloured lights.
He has a smiling expression, and gazes upon us with
    eyes of compassion.
He has four hands, the first two pressed together at
    his heart,
And the lower two holding a crystal mala and a white
    lotus flower.

He is adorned with silks and jewelled ornaments
And wears an upper garment of an antelope skin.
His crown is adorned with Amitabha.
He sits with his legs crossed in the vajra posture,
Supported from behind by a stainless moon.
He is the synthesis of all objects of refuge.

Prayer of seven limbs

With my body, speech and mind, humbly I prostrate,
And make offerings both set out and imagined.
I confess my wrong deeds from all time,
And rejoice in the virtues of all.
Please stay until samsara ceases,
And turn the Wheel of Dharma for us.
I dedicate all virtues to great enlightenment.

Offering the mandala

The ground sprinkled with perfume and spread with
    flowers,
The Great Mountain, four lands, sun and moon,
Seen as a Buddha Land and offered thus,
May all beings enjoy such Pure Lands.

Contemplating how all these pitiful migrators are my
    mothers,
Who out of kindness have cherished me again and again,
I seek your blessings to generate a spontaneous compassion
Like that of a loving mother for her dearest child.

IDAM GURU RATNA MANDALAKAM NIRYATAYAMI

Praise to Arya Avalokiteshvara

You whose white-coloured body is unstained by faults,
Whose crown is adorned with a fully enlightened Buddha,
Who gaze upon migrators with eyes of compassion,
To you Arya Avalokiteshvara I prostrate.

Requesting the five great meanings

O Arya Avalokiteshvara, Treasury of Compassion,
And all your retinue, please listen to me.

Please quickly release me and all my mothers and fathers,
The six classes of living being, from the ocean of samsara.

Please generate quickly in our mental continuum
The vast and profound Dharma of the unsurpassed
     bodhichitta.

With your compassionate nectar please purify swiftly
The karma and delusion we have accumulated since
     beginningless time.

And with your hands of compassion please swiftly lead me
And all living beings to the Pure Land of Bliss.

O Amitabha and Avalokiteshvara,
Throughout all our lives please be our Spiritual Guide;
And by perfectly revealing the unmistaken path
Please lead us all swiftly to the state of Buddhahood.

Request prayer

O Guru Avalokiteshvara, Buddha of Compassion,
Please bless my mental continuum quickly,
So that I will quickly complete
The training in purifying and transforming the six classes
of living being.

Mantra recitation

As a result of these single-pointed requests,
Light rays radiate from Arya Avalokiteshvara's body
And purify all impure karmic appearances and mistaken
awareness.
The environment becomes the Pure Land of Bliss,
And the body, speech and mind of all the inhabitants
Transform into the body, speech and mind of
Avalokiteshvara.
Everything that we know through seeing, hearing and
thinking becomes inseparable from emptiness.

OM MANI PÄME HUM

The meaning of this mantra is: with OM we are calling Avalokiteshvara, MANI means the precious jewel of enlightenment, PÄME means liberation and HUM means please bestow. Together the meaning is: 'O Avalokiteshvara, please bestow the precious jewel of enlightenment to liberate all living beings'. Through the recitation of this mantra we train in the compassionate mind of bodhichitta.

All the physical forms of myself and others are
[manifestations of] Arya Avalokiteshvara's body,
All sounds are [manifestations of] the six-letter mantra,
And all mental activity arises from great exalted wisdom.

Dedication

Through the virtues I have accumulated
By training in compassion and wisdom,
May all the impurities of the six classes of living being
be purified,
And thus may they all transform into enlightened
beings.

Prayers for the Virtuous Tradition

So that the tradition of Je Tsongkhapa,
The King of the Dharma, may flourish,
May all obstacles be pacified
And may all favourable conditions abound.

Through the two collections of myself and others
Gathered throughout the three times,
May the doctrine of Conqueror Losang Dragpa
Flourish for evermore.

The nine-line *Migtsema* prayer

Tsongkhapa, crown ornament of the scholars of the Land
of the Snows,
You are Buddha Shakyamuni and Vajradhara, the source
of all attainments,

Avalokiteshvara, the treasury of unobservable
   compassion,
Manjushri, the supreme stainless wisdom,
And Vajrapani, the destroyer of the hosts of maras.
O Venerable Guru-Buddha, synthesis of all Three Jewels,
With my body, speech, and mind, respectfully I make
   requests:
Please grant your blessings to ripen and liberate myself
   and others,
And bestow the common and supreme attainments.

(3x)

Colophon: This sadhana or ritual prayer for spiritual attainments
was translated under the compassionate guidance of Venerable
Geshe Kelsang Gyatso Rinpoche in 1978, and revised 2017

Appendix IV:
Prayers for Meditation

BRIEF PREPARATORY PRAYERS
FOR MEDITATION

Introduction

We all have the potential to gain realizations of all the stages of the path to enlightenment. These potentials are like seeds in the field of our mind, and our meditation practice is like cultivating these seeds. However, our meditation practice will be successful only if we make good preparations beforehand.

If we want to cultivate external crops, we begin by making careful preparations. First, we remove from the soil anything that might obstruct their growth, such as stones and weeds. Second, we enrich the soil with compost or fertilizer to give it the strength to sustain growth. Third, we provide warm, moist conditions to enable the seeds to germinate and the plants to grow. In the same way, to cultivate our inner crops of Dharma realizations we must also begin by making careful preparations.

First, we must purify our mind to eliminate the negative karma we have accumulated in the past, because if we do not purify this karma it will obstruct the growth of Dharma realizations. Second, we need to give our mind the strength to support the growth of Dharma realizations by accumulating merit. Third, we need to activate and sustain the growth of Dharma realizations by receiving the blessings of the holy beings.

The brief prayers that follow contain the essence of these three preparations. For more information on them, see the books *The New Meditation Handbook* or *Joyful Path of Good Fortune*.

Geshe Kelsang Gyatso
1987

Buddha Shakyamuni

Prayers for Meditation

Going for refuge

I and all sentient beings, until we achieve enlightenment,
Go for refuge to Buddha, Dharma and Sangha.

(3x, 7x, 100x, or more)

Generating bodhichitta

Through the virtues I collect by giving and other
    perfections,
May I become a Buddha for the benefit of all.

(3x)

Generating the four immeasurables

May everyone be happy,
May everyone be free from misery,
May no one ever be separated from their happiness,
May everyone have equanimity, free from hatred and
    attachment.

Visualizing the Field for Accumulating Merit

In the space before me is the living Buddha Shakyamuni
surrounded by all the Buddhas and Bodhisattvas, like the
full moon surrounded by stars.

Prayer of seven limbs

With my body, speech and mind, humbly I prostrate,
And make offerings both set out and imagined.
I confess my wrong deeds from all time,
And rejoice in the virtues of all.
Please stay until samsara ceases,
And turn the Wheel of Dharma for us.
I dedicate all virtues to great enlightenment.

Offering the mandala

The ground sprinkled with perfume and spread with
    flowers,
The Great Mountain, four lands, sun and moon,
Seen as a Buddha Land and offered thus,
May all beings enjoy such Pure Lands.

I offer without any sense of loss
The objects that give rise to my attachment, hatred
    and confusion,
My friends, enemies and strangers, our bodies and
    enjoyments;
Please accept these and bless me to be released directly
    from the three poisons.

IDAM GURU RATNA MANDALAKAM NIRYATAYAMI

Prayer of the Stages of the Path

The path begins with strong reliance
On my kind Teacher, source of all good;
O Bless me with this understanding
To follow him with great devotion.

This human life with all its freedoms,
Extremely rare, with so much meaning;
O Bless me with this understanding
All day and night to seize its essence.

My body, like a water bubble,
Decays and dies so very quickly;
After death come results of karma,
Just like the shadow of a body.

With this firm knowledge and remembrance
Bless me to be extremely cautious,
Always avoiding harmful actions
And gathering abundant virtue.

Samsara's pleasures are deceptive,
Give no contentment, only torment;
So please bless me to strive sincerely
To gain the bliss of perfect freedom.

O Bless me so that from this pure thought
Come mindfulness and greatest caution,
To keep as my essential practice
The doctrine's root, the Pratimoksha.

Just like myself all my kind mothers
Are drowning in samsara's ocean;
O So that I may soon release them,
Bless me to train in bodhichitta.

But I cannot become a Buddha
By this alone without three ethics;
So bless me with the strength to practise
The Bodhisattva's ordination.

By pacifying my distractions
And analyzing perfect meanings,
Bless me to quickly gain the union
Of special insight and quiescence.

When I become a pure container
Through common paths, bless me to enter
The essence practice of good fortune,
The supreme vehicle, Vajrayana.

The two attainments both depend on
My sacred vows and my commitments;
Bless me to understand this clearly
And keep them at the cost of my life.

By constant practice in four sessions,
The way explained by holy Teachers,
O Bless me to gain both the stages,
Which are the essence of the Tantras.

May those who guide me on the good path,
And my companions all have long lives;
Bless me to pacify completely
All obstacles, outer and inner.

May I always find perfect Teachers,
And take delight in holy Dharma,
Accomplish all grounds and paths swiftly,
And gain the state of Vajradhara.

Receiving blessings and purifying

From the hearts of all the holy beings, streams of light and nectar flow down, granting blessings and purifying.

At this point we begin the actual contemplation and meditation. After the meditation we dedicate our merit while reciting the following prayers:

Dedication prayers

Through the virtues I have collected
By practising the stages of the path,
May all living beings find the opportunity
To practise in the same way.

May everyone experience
The happiness of humans and gods,
And quickly attain enlightenment,
So that samsara is finally extinguished.

Prayers for the Virtuous Tradition

So that the tradition of Je Tsongkhapa,
The King of the Dharma, may flourish,
May all obstacles be pacified
And may all favourable conditions abound.

Through the two collections of myself and others
Gathered throughout the three times,
May the doctrine of Conqueror Losang Dragpa
Flourish for evermore.

The nine-line *Migtsema* prayer

Tsongkhapa, crown ornament of the scholars of the
     Land of the Snows,
You are Buddha Shakyamuni and Vajradhara, the
     source of all attainments,
Avalokiteshvara, the treasury of unobservable
     compassion,
Manjushri, the supreme stainless wisdom,
And Vajrapani, the destroyer of the hosts of maras.
O Venerable Guru-Buddha, synthesis of all Three Jewels,
With my body, speech and mind, respectfully I make
     requests:
Please grant your blessings to ripen and liberate myself
     and others,
And bestow the common and supreme attainments.

(3x)

Colophon: These prayers were compiled from traditional
sources by Venerable Geshe Kelsang Gyatso Rinpoche.

Appendix V:
The Blissful Path

THE CONDENSED SELF-GENERATION
SADHANA OF VAJRAYOGINI

*Those who wish to train in the self-generation of
Vajrayogini as a daily practice, but who have insufficient
time or ability to practise either the extensive or the
middling sadhana, can fulfil their aim by practising this
short sadhana with strong faith. However, whenever we
engage in the recitation, contemplation and meditation of
this sadhana,* The Blissful Path, *we should be completely
free from distractions. With distractions we cannot
accomplish anything.*

Buddha Vajradharma

THE ACTUAL SADHANA

THE FOUR PREPARATORY PRACTICES

Visualizing the objects of refuge, the gateway through which we develop and increase Buddhist faith

Faith in Buddha, Dharma and Sangha is Buddhist faith in general, and faith in Guru Vajradharma Heruka Father and Mother is Buddhist faith in particular in this practice of Vajrayogini. Guru Vajradharma Heruka Father and Mother are not different persons, but one person with different aspects. We engage in this practice following the contemplation presented in the sadhana:

In the space before me appears my root Guru in the aspect of Buddha Vajradharma, the manifestation of all Buddhas' speech, with Heruka Father and Mother at his heart, surrounded by the assembly of lineage Gurus; Yidams – the enlightened Deities; Three Precious Jewels – Buddha, Dharma and Sangha, the pure spiritual practitioners; and Dharma Protectors.

We meditate on this great assembly of enlightened holy beings with strong faith. By visualizing our root Guru in this way we will receive the special blessings of the speech of all Buddhas. Through this we can quickly attain the realizations of speech – the realizations of the Dharma instructions of Sutra and Tantra. Only through Dharma realizations can we cease our samsaric problems in general and human problems in particular.

Training in going for refuge, the gateway through which we enter Buddhism

In this practice, in order to liberate ourself and all living beings permanently from suffering, we promise from the depths of our heart to go for refuge throughout our life to the assembly of Gurus, Buddhas, Dharma and Sangha, the pure spiritual practitioners. This promise is the refuge vow, which opens the door to liberation, the supreme permanent peace of mind known as 'nirvana'. We engage in this practice following the contemplation presented in the sadhana:

I and all sentient beings as extensive as space, from now
    until we attain enlightenment,
Go for refuge to the Gurus, the supreme Spiritual Guides,
Go for refuge to the Buddhas, the fully enlightened beings,
Go for refuge to Dharma, the precious teachings of Buddha,
Go for refuge to Sangha, the pure spiritual practitioners.

(3x)

As the commitments of our refuge vow we should apply effort to receiving Buddha's blessings, to putting Dharma into practice and to receiving help from Sangha, the pure spiritual practitioners. Pure spiritual practitioners lead us to the spiritual path by showing a good example for us to follow and are therefore objects of refuge.

Generating the supreme good heart, bodhichitta, the gateway through which we enter the path to great enlightenment

In this practice, to attain enlightenment to benefit each and every living being every day, we promise from the depths of our heart to practise the stages of Vajrayogini's path, which means the stages of the paths of generation stage and completion stage of Vajrayogini. This promise is our Bodhisattva vow, which opens the door to the quick path to great enlightenment. We engage in this practice following the contemplation presented in the sadhana:

Once I have attained the state of complete enlightenment, Buddhahood, I shall free all sentient beings from the ocean of samsara's suffering and lead them to the bliss of full enlightenment. For this purpose I shall practise the stages of Vajrayogini's path.

(3x)

As the commitments of our Bodhisattva vow we should apply effort to practising the six perfections: giving, moral discipline, patience, effort, concentration and wisdom. A detailed explanation of these can be found in the book Modern Buddhism.

Receiving blessings, the gateway through which we can attain the enlightened body, speech and mind by purifying our ordinary appearance of body, speech and mind

In this practice, first we should make a short mandala offering:

The ground sprinkled with perfume and spread with
    flowers,
The Great Mountain, four lands, sun and moon,
Seen as a Buddha Land and offered thus,
May all beings enjoy such Pure Lands.

IDAM GURU RATNA MANDALAKAM NIRYATAYAMI

Then make the following request three times:

I prostrate and go for refuge to the Gurus and Three
Precious Jewels. Please bless my mental continuum.

(3x)

We then engage in the actual practice following the contemplation presented in the sadhana:

Due to requesting in this way, the great assembly of enlightened holy beings before me melts into the form of white, red and dark blue rays of light. The white rays of light are the nature of all Buddhas' bodies, the red rays of light are the nature of all Buddhas' speech, and the dark blue rays of light are the nature of all Buddhas' minds. All these dissolve into me and I receive the special blessings of all Buddhas. My ordinary appearance of body, speech and mind is purified, and my continually residing body, speech and mind transform into the enlightened body, speech and mind.

We meditate on this belief single-pointedly. Our perception of our body, speech and mind that we normally see is our ordinary appearance of body, speech and mind.

THE ACTUAL SELF-GENERATION PRACTICE

Bringing death into the path to the Truth Body, Buddha's very subtle body

In this practice, through correct imagination, we transform our clear light of death into the spiritual path of the union of great bliss and emptiness. We engage in this practice following the contemplation presented in the sadhana:

The entire world and its inhabitants melt into light and dissolve into my body. My body also melts into light and slowly diminishes in size until finally it dissolves into emptiness, the mere absence of all phenomena that I normally see. This resembles the way in which all the appearances of this life dissolve at death. I experience the clear light of death, which in nature is bliss. I perceive nothing other than emptiness. My mind, the clear light of death, becomes the union of great bliss and emptiness.

We meditate on this belief, completely free from distractions. At the end of the meditation we think:

I am Truth Body Vajrayogini.

A manifest very subtle mind at the time of death is the clear light of death. Although this contemplation and meditation is imagination, its nature is wisdom and it has inconceivable meaning. Through sincerely practising this contemplation and meditation continually, we will gain deep familiarity with transforming our clear light of death into the union of great bliss and emptiness through imagination. Then later, when we actually experience the death process, we will be able to recognize our clear light of death and transform it into the union of great bliss and emptiness. This transformation is the realization of ultimate example clear light, which will directly give us the attainment of the illusory body, a deathless body. From that moment we will become a deathless person and we will experience our world as the Pure Land of Keajra and ourself as Vajrayogini. Thus we will have fulfilled our ultimate goal. Vajrayogini imputed upon a Buddha's Truth Body is Truth Body Vajrayogini, definitive Vajrayogini.

Bringing the intermediate state into the path to the Enjoyment Body, Buddha's subtle Form Body

The state between this life and the next rebirth is the intermediate state. Beings in this state are intermediate state beings, also called 'bardo beings'. In this practice we transform the experience of an intermediate state being into the experience of Enjoyment Body Vajrayogini. Vajrayogini imputed upon a Buddha's subtle Form Body is Enjoyment Body Vajrayogini. We engage in this practice following the contemplation presented in the sadhana:

Maintaining the experience that my mind of the clear light of death has become the union of great bliss and emptiness, from the emptiness of the Truth Body, the Dharmakaya, I instantaneously transform into Enjoyment Body Vajrayogini in the form of a ball of red-coloured light, which in nature is great bliss inseparable from emptiness. This resembles the way in which the body of an intermediate state being arises out of the clear light of death. I am Enjoyment Body Vajrayogini.

We remain single-pointedly on the experience of ourself as Enjoyment Body Vajrayogini for as long as possible.

Bringing rebirth into the path to the Emanation Body, Buddha's gross Form Body

In this practice we transform our experience of taking rebirth in samsara as an ordinary being into the experience of taking rebirth in the Pure Land of Keajra as Emanation Body Vajrayogini. Vajrayogini imputed upon Buddha's gross Form Body is Emanation Body Vajrayogini. We engage in this practice following the contemplation presented in the sadhana:

In the vast space of emptiness of all phenomena, the nature of my purified mistaken appearance of all phenomena, which is the Pure Land of Keajra, I appear as Vajrayogini who is the manifestation of the wisdom of the clear light of all Buddhas. I have a red-coloured body of light, with one face and two hands, and I assume the form of a sixteen-year-old in the prime of my youth. Although I have this appearance it is not other than the emptiness of all phenomena. I am Emanation Body Vajrayogini.

We meditate on this self-generation for as long as possible with the recognition that the appearance of ourself as Vajrayogini in our Pure Land of Keajra and the emptiness of all phenomena are one entity not two. Our meditation on self-generation has the power to reduce and cease our self-grasping. In this practice we should improve our experience of training in divine pride and training in clear appearance through continually contemplating and meditating on the instructions of these trainings given in the book The New Guide to Dakini Land.

We should know that the four preparatory practices are like the four wheels of a vehicle, and the actual self-generation practice is like the vehicle itself. This shows that both the preparatory practices and the actual practice are equally important for the fulfilment of our ultimate goal.

We can train in a special inner fire, or tummo, meditation at this point. A clear and detailed explanation on how to do this can be found in the book The New Guide to Dakini Land.

Reciting the mantra

At my heart is wisdom being Vajrayogini, definitive Vajrayogini, who is the synthesis of the body, speech and mind of all Buddhas.

O My Guru Deity Vajrayogini,
Please bestow upon me and all sentient beings
The attainments of the enlightened body, speech and mind.
Please pacify our outer, inner and secret obstacles.
Please build within us the basic foundation for all
    these attainments.

For this request we recite the three-OM mantra at least as many times as we have promised.

OM OM OM SARWA BUDDHA DAKINIYE VAJRA
WARNANIYE VAJRA BEROTZANIYE HUM HUM HUM
PHAT PHAT PHAT SOHA

Outer obstacles are harm received from humans and non-humans, as well as from inanimate objects such as fire, water and so forth; inner obstacles are our delusions such as anger, attachment and ignorance; and the secret obstacle is our subtle mistaken appearance of all phenomena. Our perception of all phenomena that we normally see is our subtle mistaken appearance of all phenomena.

At this point, if we wish, we can make a tsog offering. The ritual prayer for making a tsog offering can be found in the book The New Guide to Dakini Land.

Dedication

Through the virtues I have accumulated by practising
these instructions,
May I receive the special care of Venerable Vajrayogini
and her emanation Dakinis,
And through receiving their powerful blessings upon
my very subtle body, speech and mind
May I attain enlightenment quickly to liberate all living
beings.

Prayers for the Virtuous Tradition

So that the tradition of Je Tsongkhapa,
The King of the Dharma, may flourish,
May all obstacles be pacified
And may all favourable conditions abound.

Through the two collections of myself and others
Gathered throughout the three times,
May the doctrine of Conqueror Losang Dragpa
Flourish for evermore.

The nine-line *Migtsema* prayer

Tsongkhapa, crown ornament of the scholars of the Land
    of the Snows,
You are Buddha Shakyamuni and Vajradhara, the source
    of all attainments,
Avalokiteshvara, the treasury of unobservable compassion,
Manjushri, the supreme stainless wisdom,
And Vajrapani, the destroyer of the hosts of maras.
O Venerable Guru-Buddha, synthesis of all Three Jewels,
With my body, speech and mind, respectfully I make
    requests:
Please grant your blessings to ripen and liberate myself
    and others,
And bestow the common and supreme attainments.

(3x)

Colophon: This sadhana or ritual prayer for spiritual attainments
was compiled by Venerable Geshe Kelsang Gyatso Rinpoche
from traditional sources 2012, and revised 2013.

Appendix VI:
The Eleven Yogas of Vajrayogini

THE YOGAS OF SLEEPING, RISING AND
EXPERIENCING NECTAR

Vajrayogini is a female enlightened Deity of Highest Yoga Tantra who is the manifestation of the wisdom of all Buddhas. Her function is to guide all living beings to the Pure Land of Keajra, or Dakini Land. The instructions of Vajrayogini were taught by Buddha in *Root Tantra of Heruka*. The great Yogi Naropa received these instructions directly from Vajrayogini, and passed them to Pamtingpa – one of his heart disciples. Pamtingpa then passed these instructions to the Tibetan translator Sherab Tseg, and from Sherab Tseg these instructions have been passed down in an unbroken lineage to Je Phabongkhapa, and then to the most venerable Vajradhara Trijang Rinpoche, holder of the lineage. It is from this great master that I, the author of this book, received these precious instructions.

Highest Yoga Tantra can be divided into Father Tantra and Mother Tantra. Mother Tantras principally reveal the training in clear light, which is the main cause for attaining Buddha's holy mind; and Father Tantras such as Guhyasamaja Tantra

Vajrayogini

principally reveal the training in the illusory body, which is the main cause for attaining Buddha's holy body. Because Vajrayogini Tantra is Mother Tantra, the main body of Vajrayogini practice is training in clear light. This main body has eleven limbs, which are called the 'eleven yogas'. In this context, 'yoga' means training in spiritual paths. For example, training in a spiritual path in conjunction with sleep is called the 'yoga of sleeping'.

When the eleven yogas are listed in the scriptures, the first is the yoga of sleeping. This indicates that we should begin the practice of Vajrayogini with the yoga of sleeping. As already mentioned, the main body of Vajrayogini practice is training in clear light. Clear light naturally manifests during sleep; we therefore have the opportunity to train in recognizing it during sleep. When we recognize and realize clear light directly, we will have attained meaning clear light, the realization of the fourth of the five stages of completion stage.

What is clear light? It is the very subtle mind that manifests when the inner winds enter, abide and dissolve within the central channel. Clear light is the eighth sign of the dissolution of inner winds within the central channel, and it perceives emptiness. There are three different types of clear light: (1) the clear light of sleep, (2) the clear light of death, and (3) the realization of clear light.

During sleep our very subtle mind manifests because our inner winds naturally enter and dissolve within our central channel. This very subtle mind is the clear light of sleep. It perceives emptiness, but we cannot recognize the clear light itself or emptiness because our memory cannot function during sleep. In a similar way, during our death, our very subtle mind manifests because our inner winds enter and dissolve within the central channel. This very subtle mind is the clear light of death. It perceives emptiness, but we cannot recognize the clear light itself or emptiness because our memory cannot function during death.

During waking, if we are able to cause our inner winds to enter, abide and dissolve within the central channel through the power of meditation, we experience a deep dissolution of our inner winds into the central channel, and through this our very subtle mind will manifest. This very subtle mind is the realization of clear light. Its nature is a bliss arisen from the melting of the drops inside the central channel, and its function is to prevent mistaken appearance. It is also the realization of the clear light of bliss, which is the very essence of Highest Yoga Tantra and the actual quick path to enlightenment.

In conclusion, the main body of Vajrayogini practice is training in the clear light of bliss. This can be divided into two: (1) training in bliss; and (2) training in clear light. Before training in bliss we should know what it is. This bliss is not sexual bliss; we do not need to train in sexual bliss as anyone, even an animal, can experience this without training. The bliss that we are training in is the bliss that Buddha explains in Highest Yoga Tantra. It is called 'great bliss', and possesses two special characteristics: (1) its nature is a bliss arisen from the melting of the drops inside the central channel; and (2) its function is to prevent subtle mistaken appearance. Ordinary beings cannot experience such bliss. The sexual bliss of ordinary beings arises from the melting of the drops inside the left channel, and not the central channel.

In the *Condensed Heruka Root Tantra* Buddha says:

The supreme secret of great bliss
Arises through melting the drops inside the central
    channel;
Thus it is hard to find in the world
A person who experiences such bliss.

Such a great bliss is experienced only by someone who is able to cause their inner winds to enter, abide and dissolve within their central channel through the power of meditation. Because this great bliss prevents subtle mistaken appearance, when we experience this bliss our ignorance of self-grasping and all distracting conceptual thoughts cease, and we experience a deep inner peace, which is superior to the supreme inner peace of nirvana explained by Buddha in Sutra teachings.

HOW TO PRACTISE THE YOGA OF SLEEPING

Every night when we are about to sleep we should think:

To benefit all living beings
I shall become the enlightened Buddha Vajrayogini.
For this purpose I will accomplish the realization of
    the clear light of bliss.

We then recollect that our body, our self and all other phenomena that we normally perceive do not exist. We try to perceive the mere absence of all phenomena that we normally see, the emptiness of all phenomena, and we meditate on this emptiness. Then we think and imagine:

In the vast space of emptiness of all phenomena – the Pure Land of Keajra – I appear as Vajrayogini surrounded by the enlightened Heroines and Heroes. Although I have this appearance it is not other than the emptiness of all phenomena.

We meditate on this self-generation.

We should train in this profound self-generation meditation while we are sleeping, but not in deep sleep. Through training in this practice each and every night with continual effort, gradually our memory will be able to function during sleep. Because of this, when our very subtle mind manifests during sleep we will be able to recognize or realize it. Through further training we will realize our very subtle mind directly. When this happens our mind will mix with the emptiness of all phenomena, like water mixing with water. Because of this our subtle mistaken appearance will quickly and permanently cease, and we will become an enlightened being, a Buddha. As Buddha said: 'If you realize your own mind you will become a Buddha; you should not seek Buddhahood elsewhere.' With regard to this accomplishment our sleep has so much meaning.

HOW TO PRACTISE THE YOGA OF RISING

We should try to practise the yoga of sleeping throughout the night, and throughout the day we should try to practise the yoga of rising. Every day, in the early morning, we should first meditate on the mere absence of all phenomena that we normally see or perceive, the emptiness of all phenomena. Then we think and imagine:

In the vast space of emptiness of all phenomena – the Pure
Land of Keajra – I appear as Vajrayogini surrounded by
the enlightened Heroines and Heroes. Although I have this
appearance it is not other than the emptiness of all phenomena.

We meditate on this self-generation.

We should repeat this meditation practice again and again, throughout the day. This is the yoga of rising. Then at night we again practise the yoga of sleeping. Through continually practising the cycle of the yogas of sleeping and rising, our ordinary appearances and conceptions, which are the root of our suffering, will cease.

HOW TO PRACTISE THE YOGA OF
EXPERIENCING NECTAR

Whenever we eat or drink, we should first understand and think:

For enlightened beings all food and drink are supreme nectar,
which possesses three special qualities: (1) it is medicine
nectar that cures sickness; (2) it is life nectar that prevents
death; and (3) it is wisdom nectar that pacifies delusions.

With this recognition, whenever we eat or drink we should offer our pleasure in these objects of desire to ourself, the self-generated Vajrayogini. Through practising in this way we can transform our daily experience of eating and drinking into a spiritual path that accumulates a great collection of merit, or good fortune. In the same way, whenever we enjoy seeing attractive forms or beautiful things, enjoy hearing beautiful sounds such as music or songs, enjoy smelling beautiful scents and enjoy touching tangible objects, we should offer our pleasure in these objects of desire to ourself, the self-generated Vajrayogini. In this way we can transform all our daily experiences of objects of desire into a spiritual path that leads us to the attainment of the enlightened state of Vajrayogini.

In summary, we should recognize that in the vast space of emptiness of all phenomena – the Pure Land of Keajra – is ourself Vajrayogini surrounded by the enlightened Heroines and Heroes. We should maintain this recognition through-out the day and night, except when we are concentrating on common paths, such as going for refuge, training in renunci-ation and bodhichitta, and engaging in purification practices.

This way of practising the yogas of sleeping, rising and experiencing nectar is simple but very profound. There are also other ways of practising these yogas, an explanation of which can be found in the book *The New Guide to Dakini Land*.

THE REMAINING EIGHT YOGAS

The remaining eight yogas from the yoga of immeasurables to the yoga of daily actions should be practised in conjunc-tion with the sadhana *Quick Path to Great Bliss* composed by Je Phabongkhapa. This sadhana is very blessed and precious. A detailed commentary to this sadhana and an explanation of how to practise each yoga can be found in the book *The New Guide to Dakini Land*, but the following is a brief explan-ation of their essence.

THE YOGA OF IMMEASURABLES

Going for refuge, generating bodhichitta, and meditation and recitation of Vajrasattva are called the 'yoga of immeasurables' because they are trainings in spiritual paths that will bring us immeasurable benefit in this life and countless future lives.

The meditation and recitation of Vajrasattva gives us the great opportunity to purify our mind quickly, so that we can more quickly attain enlightenment. As mentioned above, attaining enlightenment is very simple; all we need to do is apply effort to purifying our mind.

THE YOGA OF THE GURU

In this Guru yoga practice, to receive the blessings of all the Buddhas' speech we visualize our root Guru in the aspect of Buddha Vajradharma. Vajradharma, Vajradhara, Vajrasattva and Heruka are different aspects of one enlightened being. The function of Buddha Vajradharma is to bestow the blessings of all the Buddhas' speech. Through receiving these blessings, our speech will be very powerful whenever we explain Dharma instructions. In this way we can fulfil the wishes of countless living beings and purify or heal their mental continuums through the nectar of our speech.

This Guru yoga contains a practice called 'kusali tsog offering', which has the same function as the 'chod' or 'cutting' practice. It also contains a practice of receiving the blessings of the four empowerments, which will give us great confidence in accomplishing the realizations of generation and completion stages.

THE YOGA OF SELF-GENERATION

This yoga includes the practices of bringing death, the intermediate state (bardo) and rebirth into the paths to the Truth Body, Enjoyment Body and Emanation Body.

In this practice, the supporting mandala is visualized in the aspect of a double tetrahedron, which symbolizes the emptiness of all phenomena; and the supported Deities are ourself, the imagined Vajrayogini, and our retinue of Heroines.

THE YOGA OF PURIFYING MIGRATORS

In this practice, having generated ourself as the enlightened Buddha Vajrayogini, we imagine ourself giving blessings that liberate all living beings from suffering and negativities and transform them into the state of Vajrayogini – the state of ultimate happiness. This is a special practice of taking and giving according to Highest Yoga Tantra. It causes our potential to benefit directly each and every living being to ripen, and it also fulfils the commitment we made when we took the Highest Yoga Tantra empowerment in which we promised to benefit all living beings.

THE YOGA OF BEING BLESSED BY HEROES AND HEROINES

In this practice, through meditating on the body mandala of Vajrayogini, our channels and drops will receive powerful blessings directly from the thirty-seven Heroines – the female enlightened Deities of the Vajrayogini body mandala – and indirectly from their consorts, the Heroes. Also, through inviting all Heroines and Heroes (female and male enlightened beings) from the ten directions in the aspect of Vajrayogini and dissolving them into us, we will receive the blessings of all Heroes and Heroines.

The meditation on Vajrayogini's body mandala is very profound. Although it is a generation stage practice it functions to cause the inner winds to enter, abide and dissolve within the central channel. Je Phabongkhapa highly praised the practice of Vajrayogini body mandala.

THE YOGA OF VERBAL AND MENTAL RECITATION

By concentrating on verbal recitation of the Vajrayogini mantra (the 'three-OM mantra') we can accomplish the pacifying, increasing, controlling, wrathful and supreme attainments, which are mentioned in the section *Training in Mantra Recitation* of the chapter *The Practice of Heruka Body Mandala* in the book *Modern Buddhism*. The practice of mental recitation presents two completion stage meditations, both of which are the very essence of Vajrayogini practice. These two meditations are clearly explained in the book *The New Guide to Dakini Land*.

THE YOGA OF INCONCEIVABILITY

As described in the sadhana *Quick Path to Great Bliss*, having dissolved everything from the formless realm to the nada into emptiness, we imagine that we experience the clear light of bliss, and with this experience we meditate on the emptiness of all phenomena – the mere absence of all phenomena that we normally perceive. This meditation is training in the clear light of bliss, the main body of Vajrayogini practice. Through continually practising this meditation, gradually we will experience meaning clear light – the union of great bliss and emptiness – which is the actual inconceivability. In this context, 'inconceivability' means that it cannot be experienced by those who have not attained meaning clear light.

THE YOGA OF DAILY ACTIONS

The yoga of daily actions is a method for transforming all our daily actions such as eating, sleeping, working and talking into profound spiritual paths, and thus extracting great meaning from every moment of our life.

Appendix VII:
The Yoga of Buddha Heruka

THE ESSENTIAL SELF-GENERATION SADHANA
OF HERUKA BODY MANDALA
& CONDENSED SIX SESSION YOGA

Tantric commitment objects:
inner offering in kapala, vajra, bell, damaru, mala

Introduction

Those who have received the empowerment of Heruka body mandala, but who are unable to practise the extensive sadhana, *Essence of Vajrayana*, can practise this short sadhana, which contains the very essence of Heruka body mandala practice.

It is very important to improve our understanding of and faith in this precious practice through sincerely studying its commentary as presented in the book *Modern Buddhism*, in the chapter *The Practice of Heruka Body Mandala*. Having understood the meaning clearly and with strong faith we can enter, make progress on and complete the quick path to the enlightened state of Buddha Heruka.

Geshe Kelsang Gyatso
April 2010

Heruka

The Yoga of Buddha Heruka

PRELIMINARIES

Going for refuge

I and all sentient beings, until we achieve enlightenment,
Go for refuge to Buddha, Dharma and Sangha.

(3x)

Generating the supreme good heart, bodhichitta

Through the virtues I collect by giving and other
    perfections,
May I become a Buddha for the benefit of all.

(3x)

Guru yoga

VISUALIZATION AND MEDITATION

In the space before me is Guru Sumati Buddha Heruka –
Je Tsongkhapa inseparable from my root Guru, Buddha
Shakyamuni and Heruka – surrounded by all the Buddhas
of the ten directions.

INVITING THE WISDOM BEINGS

From the heart of the Protector of the hundreds of Deities of
the Joyful Land,
To the peak of a cloud which is like a cluster of fresh, white
curd,
All-knowing Losang Dragpa, King of the Dharma,
Please come to this place together with your Sons.

At this point we imagine that wisdom being Je Tsongkhapa
together with his retinue dissolves into the assembly of
Guru Sumati Buddha Heruka, and they become non-dual.

THE PRACTICE OF THE SEVEN LIMBS

In the space before me on a lion throne, lotus and moon,
The venerable Gurus smile with delight.
O Supreme Field of Merit for my mind of faith,
Please remain for a hundred aeons to spread the doctrine.

Your mind of wisdom realizes the full extent of objects of
knowledge,
Your eloquent speech is the ear-ornament of the fortunate,
Your beautiful body is ablaze with the glory of renown,
I prostrate to you, whom to see, to hear and to remember
is so meaningful.

Pleasing water offerings, various flowers,
Sweet-smelling incense, lights, scented water and so forth,
A vast cloud of offerings both set out and imagined,
I offer to you, O Supreme Field of Merit.

Whatever non-virtues of body, speech and mind
I have accumulated since time without beginning,
Especially transgressions of my three vows,
With great remorse I confess each one from the depths of
    my heart.

In this degenerate age you strove for much learning and
    accomplishment.
Abandoning the eight worldly concerns, you made your
    freedom and endowment meaningful.
O Protector, from the very depths of my heart,
I rejoice in the great wave of your deeds.

From the billowing clouds of wisdom and compassion
In the space of your Truth Body, O Venerable and holy
    Gurus,
Please send down a rain of vast and profound Dharma
Appropriate to the disciples of this world.

From your actual deathless body, born from meaning
    clear light,
Please send countless emanations throughout the world
To spread the oral lineage of the Ganden doctrine,
And may they remain for a very long time.

Through the virtues I have accumulated here,
May the doctrine and all living beings receive every
    benefit.
Especially may the essence of the doctrine
Of Venerable Losang Dragpa shine forever.

OFFERING THE MANDALA

The ground sprinkled with perfume and spread with
    flowers,
The Great Mountain, four lands, sun and moon,
Seen as a Buddha Land and offered thus,
May all beings enjoy such Pure Lands.

I offer without any sense of loss
The objects that give rise to my attachment, hatred and
    confusion,
My friends, enemies and strangers, our bodies and
    enjoyments;
Please accept these and bless me to be released directly
    from the three poisons.

IDAM GURU RATNA MANDALAKAM NIRYATAYAMI

MAKING SPECIAL REQUESTS

O Guru Sumati Buddha Heruka, from now until I attain
    enlightenment,
I shall seek no refuge other than you.
Please pacify my obstacles and bestow upon me
The two attainments of liberating and ripening.
Please bless me so that I will become definitive Heruka,
In which state I shall experience all phenomena as purified
    and gathered into emptiness, inseparable from great
    bliss.

(3x)

GENERATING THE EXPERIENCE OF GREAT BLISS AND EMPTINESS

Due to my making requests in this way, all the Buddhas of the ten directions dissolve into Je Tsongkhapa who is inseparable from my root Guru, he dissolves into Buddha Shakyamuni at his heart, and Buddha Shakyamuni dissolves into Heruka at his heart. With delight, Guru Heruka, who is the nature of the union of great bliss and emptiness, enters my body through my crown, and dissolves into my mind at my heart. Because Heruka, who is the nature of the union of great bliss and emptiness, becomes inseparable from my mind, my mind transforms into the union of great bliss and emptiness of all phenomena.

We meditate on this belief single-pointedly. This meditation is called 'training in definitive Guru yoga'. We should repeat this practice of special request and meditation again and again until we spontaneously believe that our mind has transformed into the union of great bliss and emptiness.

THE ACTUAL SELF GENERATION

In the vast space of emptiness of all phenomena, the nature of my purified mistaken appearance of all phenomena – which is the Pure Land of Keajra – I appear as Buddha Heruka with a blue-coloured body, four faces and twelve arms, the nature of my purified white indestructible drop. I am embracing Vajravarahi, the nature of my purified red indestructible drop. I am surrounded by the Heroes and Heroines of the five wheels, who are the nature of my purified subtle body – the channels and drops. I reside in the mandala, the celestial mansion, which is the nature of my purified gross body. Although I have this appearance it is not other than the emptiness of all phenomena.

At this point, (1) while experiencing great bliss and emptiness, (2) we meditate on the clear appearance of the mandala and Deities with divine pride, while (3) recognizing that the Deities are the nature of our purified channels and drops, which are our subtle body, and that the mandala is the nature of our purified gross body.

In this way we train sincerely in one single meditation on generation stage possessing these three characteristics. Holding the third characteristic – recognizing the Deities as the nature of our purified subtle body, and the mandala as the nature of our purified gross body – makes this concentration an actual body mandala meditation.

If we wish to practise completion stage meditation, we should change ourself through imagination from Heruka with four faces and twelve arms into Heruka with one face and two arms. We then engage in the meditations on the central channel, indestructible drop, indestructible wind, tummo and so forth.

Then, when we need to rest from meditation, we can practise mantra recitation.

Reciting the mantras

THE ESSENCE MANTRA OF HERUKA

At my heart is wisdom being Buddha Heruka, definitive Heruka.

O Glorious Vajra Heruka, you who enjoy
The divine illusory body and mind of clear light,
Please pacify my obstacles and bestow upon me
The two attainments of liberating and ripening.
Please bless me so that I will become definitive Heruka,
In which state I shall experience all phenomena as purified
    and gathered into emptiness, inseparable from great
    bliss.

OM SHRI VAJRA HE HE RU RU KAM HUM HUM PHAT
    DAKINI DZALA SHAMBARAM SOHA

(21x, 100x, etc.)

THE THREE-OM MANTRA OF VAJRAYOGINI

At the heart of imagined Vajrayogini (Vajravarahi) is
wisdom being Buddha Vajrayogini, definitive Vajrayogini.

OM OM OM SARWA BUDDHA DAKINIYE VAJRA
    WARNANIYE VAJRA BEROTZANIYE HUM HUM HUM
    PHAT PHAT PHAT SOHA

Recite at least as many mantras as you have promised.

*The 'three-OM' mantra is the union of the essence and close
essence mantras of Vajravarahi. The meaning of this mantra
is as follows. With OM OM OM we are calling Vajrayogini*

– the principal Deity – and her retinue of Heroines of the three wheels. SARWA BUDDHA DAKINIYE means that Vajrayogini is the synthesis of the minds of all Buddhas, VAJRA WARNANIYE means that she is the synthesis of the speech of all Buddhas, and VAJRA BEROTZANIYE means that she is the synthesis of the bodies of all Buddhas. With HUM HUM HUM we are requesting Vajrayogini and her retinues to bestow upon us the attainments of the body, speech and mind of all Buddhas. With PHAT PHAT PHAT we are requesting them to pacify our main obstacle – the subtle mistaken appearance of our body, speech and mind; and SOHA means 'please build within me the basic foundation for all these attainments'.

THE CONDENSED MANTRA OF THE SIXTY-TWO DEITIES OF HERUKA BODY MANDALA

At the heart of each of the sixty-two Deities is their individual wisdom being, their own definitive Deity.

OM HUM BAM RIM RIM LIM LIM, KAM KHAM GAM GHAM NGAM, TSAM TSHAM DZAM DZHAM NYAM, TrAM THrAM DrAM DHrAM NAM, TAM THAM DAM DHAM NAM, PAM PHAM BAM BHAM, YAM RAM LAM WAM, SHAM KAM SAM HAM HUM HUM PHAT

(7x, 21x, 100x, etc.)

When we recite this mantra we are making requests to wisdom being Buddha Heruka with Vajravarahi, and his retinue of Heroes and Heroines of the five wheels, to pacify our obstacle of subtle mistaken appearance and to

bestow upon us the attainments of outer and inner Dakini Land. Outer Dakini Land is the Pure Land of Keajra and inner Dakini Land is meaning clear light. The moment our mind is free from subtle mistaken appearance, we open the door through which we can directly see all enlightened Deities. For as long as our mind remains polluted by subtle mistaken appearance this door is closed.

Dedication

Thus, through my virtues from correctly performing
  the offerings, praises, recitations and meditations
Of the generation stage of Glorious Heruka,
May I complete all the stages
Of the common and uncommon paths.

For the sake of all living beings
May I become Heruka;
And then lead every living being
To Heruka's supreme state.

And if I do not attain this supreme state in this life,
At my deathtime may I be met by the venerable Father and
  Mother and their retinue,
With clouds of breathtaking offerings, heavenly music,
And many excellent, auspicious signs.

Then, at the end of the clear light of death,
May I be led to the Pure Land of Keajra,
The abode of the Knowledge Holders who practise the
  supreme path;
And there may I swiftly complete this profound path.

May the most profound practice and instruction of Heruka,
Practised by millions of powerful Yogis, greatly increase;
And may it remain for a very long time without
    degenerating,
As the main gateway for those seeking liberation.

May the Heroes, Dakinis and their retinues
Abiding in the twenty-four supreme places of this world,
Who possess unobstructed power for accomplishing this
    method,
Never waver from always assisting practitioners.

Auspicious prayers

May there be the auspiciousness of a great treasury of
    blessings
Arising from the excellent deeds of all the root and lineage
    Gurus,
Who have accomplished the supreme attainment of
    Buddha Heruka
By relying upon the excellent, secret path of the King of
    Tantras.

May there be the auspiciousness of the great excellent
    deeds of the Three Jewels –
The holy Buddha Jewel, the pervading nature Heruka,
    definitive Heruka;
The ultimate, great, secret Dharma Jewel, the scriptures
    and realizations of Heruka Tantra;
And the supreme Sangha Jewel, the assemblies of
    Heruka's retinue Deities.

Through all the great good fortune there is
In the precious, celestial mansions as extensive as the
  three thousand worlds,
Adorned with ornaments like the rays of the sun and
  the moon,
May all worlds and their beings have happiness,
  goodness, glory and prosperity.

Prayers for the Virtuous Tradition

So that the tradition of Je Tsongkhapa,
The King of the Dharma, may flourish,
May all obstacles be pacified
And may all favourable conditions abound.

Through the two collections of myself and others
Gathered throughout the three times,
May the doctrine of Conqueror Losang Dragpa
Flourish for evermore.

The nine-line *Migtsema* prayer

Tsongkhapa, crown ornament of the scholars of the Land
  of the Snows,
You are Buddha Shakyamuni and Vajradhara, the source
  of all attainments,
Avalokiteshvara, the treasury of unobservable
  compassion,
Manjushri, the supreme stainless wisdom,
And Vajrapani, the destroyer of the hosts of maras.
O Venerable Guru-Buddha, synthesis of all Three Jewels,

With my body, speech and mind, respectfully I make
    requests:
Please grant your blessings to ripen and liberate myself
    and others,
And bestow the common and supreme attainments.

(3x)

Condensed Six-session Yoga

Everyone who has received a Highest Yoga Tantra empowerment has a commitment to practise six-session yoga. If we are very busy, we can fulfil our six-session commitment by doing the following practice six times each day. First we recall the nineteen commitments of the five Buddha families that are listed below, and then, with a strong determination to keep these commitments purely, we recite the Condensed Six-session Yoga *that follows.*

THE NINETEEN COMMITMENTS OF THE FIVE BUDDHA FAMILIES

The six commitments of the family of Buddha Vairochana:

(1) To go for refuge to Buddha
(2) To go for refuge to Dharma
(3) To go for refuge to Sangha
(4) To refrain from non-virtue
(5) To practise virtue
(6) To benefit others

The four commitments of the family of Buddha Akshobya:

(1) To keep a vajra to remind us to emphasize the development of great bliss through meditation on the central channel

(2) To keep a bell to remind us to emphasize meditation on emptiness

(3) To generate ourself as the Deity while realizing all things that we normally see do not exist

(4) To rely sincerely upon our Spiritual Guide, who leads us to the practice of the pure moral discipline of the Pratimoksha, Bodhisattva and Tantric vows

The four commitments of the family of Buddha Ratnasambhava:

(1) To give material help

(2) To give Dharma

(3) To give fearlessness

(4) To give love

The three commitments of the family of Buddha Amitabha:

(1) To rely upon the teachings of Sutra

(2) To rely upon the teachings of the two lower classes of Tantra

(3) To rely upon the teachings of the two higher classes of Tantra

The two commitments of the family of Buddha Amoghasiddhi:

(1) To make offerings to our Spiritual Guide
(2) To strive to maintain purely all the vows we have taken

CONDENSED SIX-SESSION YOGA

I go for refuge to the Guru and Three Jewels.
Holding vajra and bell I generate as the Deity and make offerings.
I rely upon the Dharmas of Sutra and Tantra and refrain from all non-virtuous actions.
Gathering all virtuous Dharmas, I help all living beings through the practice of the four givings.

All nineteen commitments are referred to in this verse. The words, 'I go for refuge to the . . . Three Jewels', *refer to the first three commitments of the family of Buddha Vairochana – to go for refuge to Buddha, to go for refuge to Dharma and to go for refuge to Sangha. The word,* 'Guru', *refers to the fourth commitment of the family of Buddha Akshobya – to rely sincerely upon our Spiritual Guide.*

The words, 'Holding vajra and bell I generate as the Deity', *refer to the first three commitments of the family of Buddha Akshobya – to keep a vajra to remind us of great bliss, to keep a bell to remind us of emptiness, and to generate ourself as the Deity. The words,* 'and make offerings', *refer to the first commitment of the family of Buddha Amoghasiddhi – to make offerings to our Spiritual Guide.*

The words, 'I rely upon the Dharmas of Sutra and Tantra', *refer to the three commitments of the family of Buddha Amitabha – to rely upon the teachings of Sutra, to rely upon the teachings of the two lower classes of Tantra, and to rely upon the teachings of the two higher classes of Tantra. The words,* 'and refrain from all non-virtuous actions', *refer to the fourth commitment of the family of Buddha Vairochana – to refrain from non-virtue.*

The words, 'Gathering all virtuous Dharmas', *refer to the fifth commitment of the family of Buddha Vairochana – to practise virtue. The words,* 'I help all living beings', *refer to the sixth commitment of the family of Buddha Vairochana – to benefit others. The words,* 'through the practice of the four givings', *refer to the four commitments of the family of Buddha Ratnasambhava – to give material help, to give Dharma, to give fearlessness and to give love.*

Finally, the entire verse refers to the second commitment of the family of Buddha Amoghasiddhi – to strive to maintain purely all the vows we have taken.

More detail on the vows and commitments of Secret Mantra can be found in the book Tantric Grounds and Paths.

Colophon: This sadhana or ritual prayer for spiritual attainments was compiled from traditional sources by Venerable Geshe Kelsang Gyatso Rinpoche, June 2009, and revised April 2010 and December 2012.

Appendix VIII:
Offering to the Spiritual Guide

A SPECIAL WAY OF RELYING UPON
OUR SPIRITUAL GUIDE

compiled by
Losang Chokyi Gyaltsen

Introduction

Offering to the Spiritual Guide, or *Lama Chopa* in Tibetan, is a special Guru yoga of Je Tsongkhapa in conjunction with Highest Yoga Tantra. It was compiled by the first Panchen Lama, Losang Chokyi Gyaltsen, as a preliminary practice for Vajrayana Mahamudra. The main practice is relying upon the Spiritual Guide, but it also includes all the essential practices of the stages of the path (Lamrim) and training the mind (Lojong), as well as both the generation stage and completion stage of Highest Yoga Tantra.

The essence of Guru yoga is to develop a strong conviction that our Spiritual Guide is a Buddha, to make prostrations, offerings and sincere requests to him or her, and then to receive his or her profound blessings. According to the Guru yoga of *Offering to the Spiritual Guide*, we develop conviction that our Spiritual Guide is the same nature as Je Tsongkhapa, who is an emanation of the Wisdom Buddha Manjushri.

By relying upon Je Tsongkhapa, our compassion, wisdom and spiritual power naturally increase. In particular, because Je Tsongkhapa is an emanation of the Wisdom Buddha Manjushri, his faithful followers never experience difficulty in increasing their wisdom. There are many other benefits from practising *Offering to the Spiritual Guide*. These are explained in the book *Great Treasury of Merit*, which contains a complete commentary to the practice.

Offering to the Spiritual Guide can be practised privately every day, but there are two special days of each month – the 10th and the 25th – when it is recited together with making a tsog offering. In Kadampa Buddhist centres, the tsog offering on the 10th day is made to emphasize the accumulation of great merit, which is then dedicated to the long life of our Spiritual Guide; and on the 25th day the tsog offering is made to emphasize swift attainment of the realizations of the stages of the path. On each of these two days there is a different sequence of prayers, as indicated in the italicized notes interspersed throughout the text.

Geshe Kelsang Gyatso
1985

Lama Losang Tubwang Dorjechang

Offering to the Spiritual Guide

Going for refuge

With a perfectly pure mind of great virtue,
I and all mother sentient beings as extensive as space,
From now until we reach the essence of enlightenment,
Go for refuge to the Guru and Three Precious Jewels.

Namo Gurubhä
Namo Buddhaya
Namo Dharmaya
Namo Sanghaya   (3x)

Generating aspiring bodhichitta

For the sake of all mother sentient beings,
I shall become the Guru-Deity,
And then lead every sentient being
To the Guru-Deity's supreme state.   (3x)

Generating engaging bodhichitta

For the sake of all mother sentient beings I shall attain as
quickly as possible in this very life the state of the Guru-
Deity, the primordial Buddha.

I shall free all mother sentient beings from their suffering and lead them to the great bliss of the Buddha grounds. Therefore I shall practise the profound path of the yoga of the Guru-Deity.

At this point we can perform brief self-generation as our personal Deity.

Self-generation as the Deity

From the state of great bliss I arise as the Guru-Deity.

Purifying the environment and its inhabitants

Light rays radiate from my body,
Blessing all worlds and beings in the ten directions.
Everything becomes an exquisite array
Of immaculately pure good qualities.

Blessing the offerings

OM AH HUM   (3x)

By nature exalted wisdom, having the aspect of the inner offering and the individual offering substances, and functioning as objects of enjoyment of the six senses to generate a special exalted wisdom of bliss and emptiness, inconceivable clouds of outer, inner and secret offerings, commitment substances and attractive offerings cover all the ground and fill the whole of space.

Visualizing the Field of Merit

Within the vast space of indivisible bliss and emptiness,
amidst billowing clouds of Samantabhadra's offerings, fully
adorned with leaves, flowers and fruits, is a wishfulfilling
tree that grants whatever is wished for. At its crest, on a
lion throne ablaze with jewels, on a lotus, moon and sun
seat, sits my root Guru who is kind in three ways, the very
essence of all the Buddhas. He is in the aspect of a fully
ordained monk, with one face, two hands and a radiant
smile. His right hand is in the mudra of expounding
Dharma, and his left hand, in the mudra of meditative
equipoise, holds a bowl filled with nectar. He wears three
robes of resplendent saffron, and his head is graced with a
golden Pandit's hat. At his heart are Buddha Shakyamuni
and Vajradhara, who has a blue-coloured body, one face
and two hands. Holding vajra and bell, he embraces
Yingchugma and delights in the play of spontaneous bliss
and emptiness. He is adorned with many different types of
jewelled ornament and wears garments of heavenly silk.
Endowed with the major signs and minor indications, and
ablaze with a thousand rays of light, my Guru sits in the
centre of an aura of five-coloured rainbows. Sitting in the
vajra posture, his completely pure aggregates are the five
Sugatas, his four elements are the four Mothers, and his
sources, veins and joints are in reality Bodhisattvas. His
pores are the twenty-one thousand Foe Destroyers, and his
limbs are the wrathful Deities. His light rays are directional
guardians such as givers of harm and smell-eaters, and
beneath his throne are the worldly beings. Surrounding

him in sequence is a vast assembly of lineage Gurus,
Yidams, hosts of mandala Deities, Buddhas, Bodhisattvas,
Heroes, Dakinis and Dharma Protectors. Their three doors
are marked by the three vajras. Hooking light rays radiate
from the letter HUM and invite the wisdom beings from
their natural abodes to remain inseparable.

Inviting the wisdom beings

You who are the source of all happiness and goodness,
The root and lineage Gurus of the three times, the Yidams
    and Three Precious Jewels,
Together with the assembly of Heroes, Dakinis,
    Dharmapalas and Protectors,
Out of your great compassion please come to this place and
    remain firm.

Even though phenomena are by nature completely free
    from coming and going,
You appear in accordance with the dispositions of various
    disciples
And perform enlightened deeds out of wisdom and
    compassion;
O Holy Refuge and Protector, please come to this place
    together with your retinue.

OM GURU BUDDHA BODHISATTO DHARMAPALA
    SAPARIWARA EH HAYE HI: DZA HUM BAM HO
The wisdom beings become inseparable from the
    commitment beings.

Prostrating to the Spiritual Guide as the Enjoyment Body

Spiritual Guide with a jewel-like form,
Who out of compassion bestow in an instant
Even the supreme state of the three bodies, the sphere of
    great bliss,
O Vajra Holder I prostrate at your lotus feet.

Prostrating to the Spiritual Guide as the Emanation Body

Exalted wisdom of all the infinite Conquerors
Out of supremely skilful means appearing to suit disciples,
Now assuming the form of a saffron-robed monk,
O Holy Refuge and Protector I prostrate at your lotus feet.

Prostrating to the Spiritual Guide as the Truth Body

Abandonment of all faults together with their imprints,
Precious treasury of countless good qualities,
And sole gateway to all benefit and happiness,
O Venerable Spiritual Guide I prostrate at your lotus feet.

Prostrating to the Spiritual Guides as the synthesis of all Three Jewels

Essence of all Guru-Buddhas and Deities,
Source of all eighty-four thousand classes of holy Dharma,
Foremost amongst the entire Superior Assembly,
O Kind Spiritual Guides I prostrate at your lotus feet.

Prostrating to the lineage Gurus and Three Jewels

To the Gurus who abide in the three times and the ten
    directions,
The Three Supreme Jewels, and all other objects of
    prostration,
I prostrate with faith and respect, a melodious chorus of
    praise,
And emanated bodies as numerous as atoms in the world.

Offering the outer offerings and the five objects of desire

O Guru, Refuge and Protector, together with your retinue,
I offer you these vast clouds of various offerings:

The purifying nectars of the four waters gently flowing
From expansive and radiant jewelled vessels perfectly
    arrayed;

Beautiful flowers, petals and garlands finely arranged,
Covering the ground and filling the sky;

The lapis-coloured smoke of fragrant incense
Billowing in the heavens like blue summer clouds;

The playful light of the sun and the moon, glittering jewels
    and a vast array of lamps
Dispelling the darkness of the three thousand worlds;

Exquisite perfume scented with camphor, sandalwood
    and saffron,
In a vast swirling ocean stretching as far as the eye can
    see;

Nutritious food and drink endowed with a hundred
 flavours
And delicacies of gods and men heaped as high as a
 mountain;

From an endless variety of musical instruments,
Melodious tunes filling all three worlds;

Delightful bearers of forms, sounds, smells, tastes and
 objects of touch –
Goddesses of outer and inner enjoyments filling all
 directions.

Offering the mandala

O Treasure of Compassion, my Refuge and Protector,
 supremely perfect Field of Merit,
With a mind of devotion I offer to you
A thousand million of the Great Mountain, the four
 continents,
The seven major and minor royal possessions, and so
 forth,
A collection of perfect worlds and beings that give rise
 to all joys,
A great treasury of the desired enjoyments of gods and
 men.

Offering our spiritual practice

O Venerable Guru, I offer these pleasure gardens,
Both actually arranged and emanated by mind, on the
 shores of a wish-granting sea,

In which, from the pure white virtues of samsara and
    nirvana,
There arise offering substances of broad, thousand-petalled
    lotuses that delight the minds of all;
Where my own and others' mundane and supramundane
    virtues of the three doors
Are flowers that bring colour to every part
And emit a multitude of scents like Samantabhadra's
    offerings;
And where the three trainings, the five paths and the two
    stages are the fruit.

Inner offering

I offer this ocean of nectar with the five hooks, the five
    lamps, and so forth,
Purified, transformed and increased,
Together with a drink of excellent tea
Endowed with a hundred flavours, the radiance of saffron
    and a delicate aroma.

*During a long life puja, on the 10th day of the month, it
is customary at this point to make a tea offering, while
reciting the following verse:*

The Guru is Buddha, the Guru is Dharma,
The Guru is also Sangha.
The Guru is the source of all joys;
To all Gurus I make this offering.
OM AH HUM   (3x)

If we wish to make a tsog offering to emphasize the accumulation of great merit, such as on the 10th day of the month, we should do so at this point. The tsog offering is on page 235.

Secret offering

And I offer most attractive illusory mudras,
A host of messengers born from places, born from mantra
 and spontaneously born,
With slender bodies, skilled in the sixty-four arts of love,
And possessing the splendour of youthful beauty.

Thatness offering

I offer you the supreme, ultimate bodhichitta,
A great, exalted wisdom of spontaneous bliss free from
 obstructions,
Inseparable from the nature of all phenomena, the sphere
 of freedom from elaboration,
Effortless, and beyond words, thoughts and expressions.

Offering medicines, and ourself as a servant

I offer many different types of excellent medicine
That destroy the four hundred and four diseases of the
 delusions,
And to please you I offer myself as a servant;
Please keep me in your service for as long as space exists.

If we wish, we may recite the Mahayana Sutra of the Three Superior Heaps *at this point.*

If we wish to make a tsog offering to emphasize purification, we should do so at this point. The tsog offering is on page 235.

Confession

In the presence of the great Compassionate Ones I confess
    with a mind of great regret
All the non-virtues and negative actions that, since
    beginningless time,
I have done, ordered to be done, or rejoiced in;
And I promise that from now on I shall not commit them
    again.

Rejoicing

Though phenomena have no sign of inherent existence,
From the depths of our hearts we rejoice
In all the dream-like happiness and pure white virtue
That arise for ordinary and Superior beings.

Requesting the turning of the Wheel of Dharma

From the myriads of billowing clouds of your sublime
    wisdom and compassion,
Please send down a rain of vast and profound Dharma,
So that in the jasmine garden of benefit and happiness
There may be growth, sustenance and increase for all these
    living beings.

Beseeching the Spiritual Guide not to pass away

In a long life puja, on the 10th day of the month, it is customary at this point to make a special mandala offering (see page 247), to recite special prayers for the long life of our Spiritual Guide and to recite the following verse three times:

Though your vajra body has no birth or death,
We request the vessel of the great King of Union
To remain unchanging according to our wishes,
Without passing away until samsara ends.

Dedication

I dedicate all the pure white virtues I have gathered here, so
    that in all my lives
I shall never be separated from the venerable Guru who is
    kind in three ways;
May I always come under his loving care,
And attain the Union of Vajradhara.

It is customary to recite the nine-line Migtsema *prayer at this point:*

The nine-line *Migtsema* prayer

Tsongkhapa, crown ornament of the scholars of the Land
    of the Snows,
You are Buddha Shakyamuni and Vajradhara, the source
    of all attainments,
Avalokiteshvara, the treasury of unobservable compassion,
Manjushri, the supreme stainless wisdom,

And Vajrapani, the destroyer of the hosts of maras.
O Venerable Guru-Buddha, synthesis of all Three Jewels,
With my body, speech and mind, respectfully I make
    requests:
Please grant your blessings to ripen and liberate myself and
    others,
And bestow the common and supreme attainments.

(3x)

*If we wish to make a mandala offering together with
the three great requests we may do so at this point. The
mandala offering is on page 245.*

*Also, if we wish to receive blessings so as to gain
Mahamudra realizations, we may recite the* Prayers of
Request to the Mahamudra Lineage Gurus *and/or* The
Condensed Meaning of the Swift Vajrayana Path *at
this point. These can be found in the commentary* Great
Treasury of Merit.

Requesting by remembering his good qualities as explained in the Vinaya scriptures

Great ocean of moral discipline, source of all good qualities,
Replete with a collection of jewels of extensive learning,
Second Buddha, venerable saffron-robed monk,
O Elder and Holder of the Vinaya, to you I make requests.

Requesting by remembering his good qualities as a Mahayana Spiritual Guide

You who possess the ten qualities
Of an authentic Teacher of the path of the Sugatas,

Lord of the Dharma, representative of all the Conquerors,
O Mahayana Spiritual Guide, to you I make requests.

Requesting by remembering his good qualities as a Vajrayana Spiritual Guide

Your three doors are perfectly controlled, you have great
    wisdom and patience,
You are without pretension or deceit, you are well-versed in
    mantras and Tantra,
You possess the two sets of ten qualities, and you are
    skilled in drawing and explaining,
O Principal Holder of the Vajra, to you I make requests.

Requesting by remembering that he is kinder than all the Buddhas

To the coarse beings of these impure times who, being so
    hard to tame,
Were not subdued by the countless Buddhas of old,
You correctly reveal the excellent path of the Sugatas;
O Compassionate Refuge and Protector, to you I make
    requests.

Requesting by remembering that he is kinder even than Buddha Shakyamuni

Now, when the sun of Buddha has set,
For the countless migrators without protection or refuge
You perform exactly the same deeds as the Conqueror;
O Compassionate Refuge and Protector, to you I make
    requests.

Requesting by remembering that he is a supreme Field of Merit

Even just one of your hair pores is praised for us
As a Field of Merit that is superior to all the Conquerors
Of the three times and the ten directions;
O Compassionate Refuge and Protector, to you I make
　　requests.

Requesting by expressing his outer qualities

From the play of your miracle powers and skilful means
The ornament wheels of your three Sugata bodies
Appear in an ordinary form to guide migrators;
O Compassionate Refuge and Protector, to you I make
　　requests.

Requesting by expressing his inner qualities

Your aggregates, elements, sources and limbs
Are by nature the Fathers and Mothers of the five Buddha
　　families,
The Bodhisattvas and the Wrathful Deities;
O Supreme Spiritual Guide, the nature of the Three Jewels,
　　to you I make requests.

Requesting by expressing his secret qualities

You are the essence of the ten million circles of mandalas
That arise from the state of the all-knowing exalted
　　wisdom;
Principal Holder of the Vajra, pervasive source of the
　　hundred families,

O Protector of the Primordial Union, to you I make
    requests.

Requesting by expressing his thatness qualities

Pervasive nature of all things stable and moving,
Inseparable from the experience of spontaneous joy
    without obstructions;
Thoroughly good, from the beginning free from extremes,
O Actual, ultimate bodhichitta, to you I make requests.

Single-pointed request

You are the Guru, you are the Yidam, you are the Daka
    and Dharma Protector;
From now until I attain enlightenment I shall seek no
    refuge other than you.
In this life, in the bardo, and until the end of my lives,
    please hold me with the hook of your compassion,
Liberate me from the fears of samsara and peace, bestow
    all the attainments, be my constant companion, and
    protect me from all obstacles.

(3x)

Receiving the blessings of the four empowerments

Through the force of requesting three times in this way,
white, red, and blue light rays and nectars, serially and
together, arise from the places of my Guru's body, speech
and mind, and dissolve into my three places, serially and
together. My four obstructions are purified and I receive
the four empowerments. I attain the four bodies and, out

221

of delight, an emanation of my Guru dissolves into me and bestows his blessings.

At this point we meditate briefly on receiving the blessings of the four empowerments according to the commentary, Great Treasury of Merit. *Then we imagine that an emanation of Lama Losang Tubwang Dorjechang comes to the crown of our head and, entering into our central channel, descends to our heart. We imagine that our subtle body, speech and mind become of one taste with our Spiritual Guide's body, speech and mind, and meditate on this special feeling of bliss for a while. After this we recite the mantras according to the commentary.*

On the 25th day of the month, it is customary at this point to make a tea offering, while reciting4 the following verse:

The Guru is Buddha, the Guru is Dharma,
The Guru is also Sangha.
The Guru is the source of all joys;
To all Gurus I make this offering.
OM AH HUM   (3x)

If we wish to make a tsog offering to emphasize the swift attainment of the realizations of the stages of the path, such as on the 25th day of the month, we should do so here. The tsog offering is on page 235.

If we wish to offer a long mandala to request the realizations of the stages of the path, such as on the 25th day of the month, we should do so here. The mandala offering is on page 245.

Request Prayer of the Stages of the Path

How to rely upon our Spiritual Guide, the root of spiritual paths

Through the force of my making offerings and respectful
    requests
To the venerable Spiritual Guide, the holy, supreme Field
    of Merit,
I seek your blessings, O Protector, the root of all goodness
    and joy,
So that you will gladly take me into your loving care.

Developing the aspiration to take the essence of our human life

Realizing that this freedom and endowment, found only
    once,
Are difficult to attain, and yet decay so quickly,
I seek your blessings to seize their essential meaning,
Undistracted by the meaningless activities of this life.

The actual method for gaining the happiness of higher states in future lives

Fearing the blazing fires of the sufferings of bad
    migrations,
From the depths of my heart I go for refuge to the Three
    Jewels,
And seek your blessings to strive sincerely
To abandon non-virtue and practise the entire collection
    of virtue.

Developing the wish to gain liberation

Being violently tossed by the waves of delusion and karma
And tormented by the sea-monsters of the three sufferings,
I seek your blessings to develop a strong wish for liberation
From the boundless and fearful great ocean of samsara.

How to practise the path that leads to liberation

Forsaking the mind that views as a pleasure garden
This unbearable prison of samsara,
I seek your blessings to take up the victory banner of
    liberation
By maintaining the three higher trainings and the wealths
    of Superiors.

How to generate great compassion, the foundation of the
    Mahayana

Contemplating how all these pitiful migrators are my
    mothers,
Who out of kindness have cherished me again and again,
I seek your blessings to generate a spontaneous compassion
Like that of a loving mother for her dearest child.

Equalizing self and others

In that no one wishes for even the slightest suffering,
Or is ever content with the happiness they have,
There is no difference between myself and others;
Realizing this, I seek your blessings joyfully to make
    others happy.

The dangers of self-cherishing

Seeing that this chronic disease of cherishing myself
Is the cause that gives rise to unwanted suffering,
I seek your blessings to destroy this great demon of
    selfishness
By resenting it as the object of blame.

The benefits of cherishing others

Seeing that the mind that cherishes mother beings and
    would secure their happiness
Is the gateway that leads to infinite good qualities,
I seek your blessings to cherish these beings more than my
    life,
Even if they rise up against me as my enemies.

Exchanging self with others

In short, since the childish are concerned for themselves
    alone,
Whereas Buddhas work solely for the sake of others,
I seek your blessings to distinguish the faults and benefits,
And thus be able to exchange myself with others.

Since cherishing myself is the door to all faults
And cherishing mother beings is the foundation of all good
    qualities,
I seek your blessings to take as my essential practice
The yoga of exchanging self with others.

Taking and giving

Therefore, O Compassionate, Venerable Guru, I seek your
    blessings
So that all the suffering, negativities and obstructions of
    mother sentient beings
Will ripen upon me right now;
And through my giving my happiness and virtue to
    others,
May all migrating beings be happy.   (3x)

The third to the seventh points of training the mind

Though the world and its beings, filled with the effects of
    evil,
Pour down unwanted suffering like rain,
This is a chance to exhaust the effects of negative actions;
Seeing this, I seek your blessings to transform adverse
    conditions into the path.

In short, whether favourable or unfavourable conditions
    arise,
I seek your blessings to transform them into the path of
    improving the two bodhichittas
Through practising the five forces, the essence of all
    Dharmas,
And thereby maintain a happy mind alone.

I seek your blessings to make this freedom and endowment
    extremely meaningful
By immediately applying meditation to whatever I meet
Through the skilful means of the four preparations,

And by practising the commitments and precepts of
   training the mind.

How to meditate on superior intention and generate
   bodhichitta

Through love, compassion and superior intention,
And the magical practice of mounting taking and giving
   upon the breath,
I seek your blessings to generate the actual bodhichitta,
To free all migrators from this great ocean of samsara.

How to take the vows of aspiring and engaging
   bodhichitta

I seek your blessings to strive sincerely on the sole path
Traversed by all the Conquerors of the three times –
To bind my mind with pure Bodhisattva vows
And practise the three moral disciplines of the Mahayana.

*At this point we can send out the remainder of the tsog
offering to the spirits. See pages 242-243.*

How to practise the perfection of giving

I seek your blessings to complete the perfection of giving
Through the instructions on improving the mind of giving
   without attachment,
And thus to transform my body, my enjoyments, and my
   virtues amassed throughout the three times
Into whatever each sentient being desires.

How to practise the perfection of moral discipline

I seek your blessings to complete the perfection of moral
    discipline
By not transgressing even at the cost of my life
The discipline of the Pratimoksha, Bodhisattva and Secret
    Mantra vows,
And by gathering virtuous Dharmas, and accomplishing
    the welfare of sentient beings.

How to practise the perfection of patience

I seek your blessings to complete the perfection of patience
So that even if every single being in the three realms,
Out of anger were to abuse me, criticize me, threaten me, or
    even take my life,
Undisturbed, I would repay their harm by helping them.

How to practise the perfection of effort

I seek your blessings to complete the perfection of effort
By striving for supreme enlightenment with unwavering
    compassion;
Even if I must remain in the fires of the deepest hell
For many aeons for the sake of each being.

How to practise the perfection of mental stabilization

I seek your blessings to complete the perfection of mental
    stabilization
By abandoning the faults of mental sinking, mental
    excitement and mental wandering,

And concentrating in single-pointed absorption
On the state that is the lack of true existence of all
　　phenomena.

How to practise the perfection of wisdom by sustaining space-like meditative equipoise

I seek your blessings to complete the perfection of wisdom
Through the yoga of the space-like meditative equipoise on
　　the ultimate,
With the great bliss of the suppleness
Induced by the wisdom of individual analysis of thatness.

How to practise the perfection of wisdom by sustaining illusion-like subsequent attainment

Outer and inner phenomena are like illusions, like dreams,
And like reflections of the moon in a clear lake,
For though they appear they do not truly exist;
Realizing this, I seek your blessings to complete the
　　illusion-like concentration.

How to train the mind in the profound view of the middle way

I seek your blessings to realize the meaning of Nagarjuna's
　　intention,
That there is no contradiction but only harmony
Between the absence of even an atom of inherent existence
　　in samsara and nirvana
And the non-deceptive dependent relationship of cause
　　and effect.

Becoming a suitable vessel for the profound path of Secret Mantra, and keeping the vows and commitments purely

And then the swirling ocean of the Tantras is crossed
Through the kindness of the navigator, the Vajra Holder.
I seek your blessings to cherish more than my life
The vows and commitments, the root of attainments.

How to meditate on generation stage

Through the yoga of the first stage that transforms birth,
    death and bardo
Into the three bodies of the Conquerors,
I seek your blessings to purify all stains of ordinary
    appearance and conception,
And to see whatever appears as the form of the Deity.

How to practise completion stage

I seek your blessings, O Protector, that you may place your
    feet
On the centre of the eight-petalled lotus at my heart,
So that I may manifest within this life
The paths of illusory body, clear light and union.

The way to practise the ritual of the transference of consciousness if, having meditated, we have received no signs

If by the time of my death I have not completed the path,
I seek your blessings to go to the Pure Land

Through the instruction on correctly applying the five
    forces,
The supremely powerful method of transference to
    Buddhahood.

How to offer prayers to be cared for by our Spiritual Guide in all future lives

In short, O Protector, I seek your blessings so that
    throughout all my lives
I shall never be separated from you, but always come under
    your care;
And as the foremost of your disciples,
Maintain all the secrets of your body, speech and mind.

O Protector, wherever you manifest as a Buddha,
May I be the very first in your retinue;
And may everything be auspicious for me to accomplish
    without effort
All temporary and ultimate needs and wishes.

Gathering and dissolving the Field of Merit

*It is customary not to recite the following verse during a
long life puja, such as on the 10th day of the month:*

Due to my making requests in this way, O Supreme
    Spiritual Guide,
With delight, please come to my crown to bestow your
    blessings;
And once again firmly place your radiant feet
On the anthers of the lotus at my heart.

At this point we can train in the practice of Vajrayana Mahamudra, the actual completion stage meditation, according to the commentary.

Dedication

I dedicate all the pure white virtues I have gathered here
So that I may accomplish all the prayers
Made by the Sugatas and Bodhisattvas of the three times,
And maintain the holy Dharma of scripture and insight.

Through the force of this, throughout all my lives,
May I never be separated from the four wheels of the
    Supreme Vehicle,
And thus may I complete the paths of renunciation,
Bodhichitta, correct view, and the two Tantric stages.

Auspicious prayers

Through the force of all the pure white virtue in samsara
    and nirvana,
Henceforth may there be a celestial treasury of temporary
    and ultimate goodness and joy,
Free from all stains of inauspiciousness;
And thus may there be the auspiciousness of enjoying
    magnificent delight.

May the Dharma Centres of all-knowing Losang Dragpa
Be filled with hosts of Sangha and Yogis
Striving to practise single-pointedly the three pure
    trainings;
And thus may there be the auspiciousness of Buddha's
    doctrine remaining for a very long time.

Abiding in the blessings of Losang Dragpa,
Who from the time of his youth made requests to the
    supreme Guru-Deity,
May we effortlessly accomplish the welfare of others;
And thus may there be the auspiciousness of Losang
    Dorjechang.

May desired endowments increase like a summer lake,
May we find uninterrupted birth with freedom in stainless
    families,
May we pass each day and night with Losang's holy
    Dharma;
And thus may there be the auspiciousness of enjoying
    magnificent delight.

From now until I and others attain enlightenment,
Through the virtues we have already created and will
    create,
May there be the auspiciousness of the Venerable Guru's
    holy form
Remaining like an immutable vajra in this world.

Prayers for the Virtuous Tradition

So that the tradition of Je Tsongkhapa,
The King of the Dharma, may flourish,
May all obstacles be pacified
And may all favourable conditions abound.

Through the two collections of myself and others
Gathered throughout the three times,
May the doctrine of Conqueror Losang Dragpa
Flourish for evermore.

The nine-line *Migtsema* prayer

Tsongkhapa, crown ornament of the scholars of the Land of the Snows,

You are Buddha Shakyamuni and Vajradhara, the source of all attainments,

Avalokiteshvara, the treasury of unobservable compassion,

Manjushri, the supreme stainless wisdom,

And Vajrapani, the destroyer of the hosts of maras.

O Venerable Guru-Buddha, synthesis of all Three Jewels,

With my body, speech and mind, respectfully I make requests:

Please grant your blessings to ripen and liberate myself and others,

And bestow the common and supreme attainments.

(3x)

The Tsog Offering

Blessing the offering substances

OM AH HUM   (3x)

By nature exalted wisdom, having the aspect of the inner
offering and the individual offering substances, and
functioning as objects of enjoyment of the six senses to
generate a special, exalted wisdom of bliss and emptiness,
inconceivable clouds of outer, inner and secret offerings,
commitment substances and attractive offerings, cover all
the ground and fill the whole of space.

EH MA HO Great manifestation of exalted wisdom.
All realms are vajra realms
And all places are great vajra palaces
Endowed with vast clouds of Samantabhadra's offerings,
An abundance of all desired enjoyments.
All beings are actual Heroes and Heroines.
Everything is immaculately pure,
Without even the name of mistaken impure appearance.

HUM All elaborations are completely pacified in the state
of the Truth Body. The wind blows and the fire blazes.
Above, on a grate of three human heads, AH within a
qualified skullcup, OM the individual substances blaze.

Above these stand OM AH HUM, each ablaze with its brilliant colour. Through the wind blowing and the fire blazing, the substances melt. Boiling, they swirl in a great vapour. Masses of light rays from the three letters radiate to the ten directions and invite the three vajras together with nectars. These dissolve separately into the three letters. Melting into nectar, they blend with the mixture. Purified, transformed, and increased,
EH MA HO They become a blazing ocean of magnificent delights.

OM AH HUM   (3x)

Inviting the guests of the tsog offering

O Root and lineage Gurus, whose nature is compassion,
The assembly of Yidams and objects of refuge, the Three
    Precious Jewels,
And the hosts of Heroes, Dakinis, Dharma Protectors and
    Dharmapalas,
I invite you, please come to this place of offerings.

Amidst vast clouds of outer, inner and secret offerings,
With light radiating even from your feet,
O Supremely Accomplished One please remain firm on
    this beautiful throne of jewels
And bestow the attainments that we long for.

Making the tsog offering

HO This ocean of tsog offering of uncontaminated nectar,
Blessed by concentration, mantra and mudra,

I offer to please the assembly of root and lineage Gurus.
OM AH HUM
Delighted by enjoying these magnificent objects of desire,
EH MA HO
Please bestow a great rain of blessings.

HO This ocean of tsog offering of uncontaminated nectar,
Blessed by concentration, mantra and mudra,
I offer to please the divine assembly of Yidams and their
retinues.
OM AH HUM
Delighted by enjoying these magnificent objects of desire,
EH MA HO
Please bestow a great rain of attainments.

HO This ocean of tsog offering of uncontaminated nectar,
Blessed by concentration, mantra and mudra,
I offer to please the assembly of Three Precious Jewels.
OM AH HUM
Delighted by enjoying these magnificent objects of desire,
EH MA HO
Please bestow a great rain of sacred Dharmas.

HO This ocean of tsog offering of uncontaminated nectar,
Blessed by concentration, mantra and mudra,
I offer to please the assembly of Dakinis and Dharma
Protectors.
OM AH HUM
Delighted by enjoying these magnificent objects of desire,
EH MA HO
Please bestow a great rain of virtuous deeds.

HO This ocean of tsog offering of uncontaminated nectar,
Blessed by concentration, mantra and mudra,
I offer to please the assembly of mother sentient beings.
OM AH HUM
Delighted by enjoying these magnificent objects of desire,
EH MA HO
May suffering and mistaken appearance be pacified.

Making the tsog offering to the Vajrayana Spiritual Guide

EH MA HO Great circle of tsog!
O Great Hero we understand
That, following in the path of the Sugatas of the three times,
You are the source of all attainments.
Forsaking all minds of conceptualization
Please continuously enjoy this circle of tsog.
AH LA LA HO

The Vajrayana Spiritual Guide's reply

OM With a nature inseparable from the three vajras
I generate as the Guru-Deity.
AH This nectar of uncontaminated exalted wisdom and
    bliss,
HUM Without stirring from bodhichitta
I partake to delight the Deities dwelling in my body.
AH HO MAHA SUKHA

*It is customary at this point to recite special prayers for the
long life of our Spiritual Guide.*

Song of the Spring Queen

HUM All you Tathagatas,
Heroes, Yoginis,
Dakas and Dakinis,
To all of you I make this request:
O Heruka who delight in great bliss,
You engage in the Union of spontaneous bliss,
By attending the Lady intoxicated with bliss
And enjoying in accordance with the rituals.
AH LA LA, LA LA HO, AH I AH, AH RA LI HO
May the assembly of stainless Dakinis
Look with loving affection and accomplish all deeds.

HUM All you Tathagatas,
Heroes, Yoginis,
Dakas and Dakinis,
To all of you I make this request:
With a mind completely aroused by great bliss
And a body in a dance of constant motion,
I offer to the hosts of Dakinis
The great bliss from enjoying the lotus of the mudra.
AH LA LA, LA LA HO, AH I AH, AH RA LI HO
May the assembly of stainless Dakinis
Look with loving affection and accomplish all deeds.

HUM All you Tathagatas,
Heroes, Yoginis,
Dakas and Dakinis,
To all of you I make this request:
You who dance with a beautiful and peaceful manner,

O Blissful Protector and the hosts of Dakinis,
Please come here before me and grant me your blessings,
And bestow upon me spontaneous great bliss.
AH LA LA, LA LA HO, AH I AH, AH RA LI HO
May the assembly of stainless Dakinis
Look with loving affection and accomplish all deeds.

HUM All you Tathagatas,
Heroes, Yoginis,
Dakas and Dakinis,
To all of you I make this request:
You who have the characteristic of the liberation of great
    bliss,
Do not say that deliverance can be gained in one lifetime
Through various ascetic practices having abandoned
great bliss,
But that great bliss resides in the centre of the supreme
    lotus.
AH LA LA, LA LA HO, AH I AH, AH RA LI HO
May the assembly of stainless Dakinis
Look with loving affection and accomplish all deeds.

HUM All you Tathagatas,
Heroes, Yoginis,
Dakas and Dakinis,
To all of you I make this request:
Like a lotus born from the centre of a swamp,
This method, though born from attachment, is unstained by
    the faults of attachment.
O Supreme Dakini, through the bliss of your lotus,
Please quickly bring liberation from the bonds of samsara.

AH LA LA, LA LA HO, AH I AH, AH RA LI HO
May the assembly of stainless Dakinis
Look with loving affection and accomplish all deeds.

HUM All you Tathagatas,
Heroes, Yoginis,
Dakas and Dakinis,
To all of you I make this request:
Just as the essence of honey in the honey source
Is drunk by swarms of bees from all directions,
So through your broad lotus with six characteristics
Please bring satisfaction with the taste of great bliss.
AH LA LA, LA LA HO, AH I AH, AH RA LI HO
May the assembly of stainless Dakinis
Look with loving affection and accomplish all deeds.

Return to page 215 on the 10th of the month, when making a tsog offering to emphasize the accumulation of great merit, such as a long life puja.

Return to page 216 when making a tsog offering to emphasize purification.

Return to page 223 on the 25th of the month, when making a tsog offering to emphasize the attainment of the stages of the path.

Blessing the remaining tsog offering

HUM Impure mistaken appearances are purified in
    emptiness,
AH Great nectar accomplished from exalted wisdom,
OM It becomes a vast ocean of desired enjoyment.
OM AH HUM   (3x)

Giving the remaining tsog offering to the spirits

HO This ocean of remaining tsog offering of
    uncontaminated nectar,
Blessed by concentration, mantra and mudra,
I offer to please the assembly of oath-bound guardians.
OM AH HUM
Delighted by enjoying these magnificent objects of desire,
EH MA HO
Please perform perfect actions to help practitioners.

Send out the remainder of the tsog offering to the spirits.

HO
O Guests of the remainder together with your retinues
Please enjoy this ocean of remaining tsog offering.
May those who spread the precious doctrine,
The holders of the doctrine, their benefactors, and others,
And especially I and other practitioners
Have good health, long life, power,
Glory, fame, fortune,
And extensive enjoyments.
Please grant me the attainments
Of pacifying, increasing, controlling and wrathful actions.
You who are bound by oaths please protect me
And help me to accomplish all the attainments.
Eradicate all untimely death, sicknesses,
Harm from spirits and hindrances.
Eliminate bad dreams,
Ill omens and bad actions.

May there be happiness in the world, may the years be
    good,
May crops increase, and may the Dharma flourish.
May all goodness and happiness come about,
And may all wishes be accomplished.

By the force of this bountiful giving
May I become a Buddha for the sake of living beings;
And through my generosity may I liberate
All those not liberated by previous Buddhas.

Return to page 227.

Colophon: This sadhana or ritual prayer for relying upon
our Spiritual Guide was translated under the compassionate
guidance of Venerable Geshe Kelsang Gyatso Rinpoche.

Offering the Mandala

OM VAJRA BHUMI AH HUM
Great and powerful golden ground,
OM VAJRA REKHE AH HUM
At the edge the iron fence stands around the outer circle.
In the centre Mount Meru the king of mountains,
Around which are four continents:
In the east, Purvavideha, in the south, Jambudipa,
In the west, Aparagodaniya, in the north, Uttarakuru.
Each has two sub-continents:
Deha and Videha, Tsamara and Abatsamara,
Satha and Uttaramantrina, Kurava and Kaurava.
The mountain of jewels, the wish-granting tree,
The wish-granting cow, and the harvest unsown.
The precious wheel, the precious jewel,
The precious queen, the precious minister,
The precious elephant, the precious supreme horse,
The precious general, and the great treasure vase.
The goddess of beauty, the goddess of garlands,
The goddess of song, the goddess of dance,
The goddess of flowers, the goddess of incense,
The goddess of light, and the goddess of scent.
The sun and the moon, the precious umbrella,
The banner of victory in every direction.

In the centre all treasures of both gods and men,
An excellent collection with nothing left out.
I offer this to you my kind root Guru and lineage Gurus,
To all of you sacred and glorious Gurus;
And especially to you, great Lama Losang Tubwang
    Dorjechang together with your retinues.
Please accept with compassion for migrating beings,
And having accepted, out of your great compassion,
Please bestow your blessings on all sentient beings
    pervading space.

The ground sprinkled with perfume and spread with
    flowers,
The Great Mountain, four lands, sun and moon,
Seen as a Buddha Land and offered thus,
May all beings enjoy such Pure Lands.

I offer without any sense of loss
The objects that give rise to my attachment, hatred and
    confusion,
My friends, enemies and strangers, our bodies and
    enjoyments;
Please accept these and bless me to be released directly
    from the three poisons.

IDAM GURU RATNA MANDALAKAM NIRYATAYAMI

*On the 25th of the month, when making a mandala offering
to request realizations of the stages of the path, return to
page 223.*

*When making a mandala offering together with the three
great requests return to page 218.*

Mandala Offering Requesting the Guru to Remain

First the chant leader recites the following:

O Glorious and sacred Guru whose nature is inseparable from the Great Conqueror, the all-pervasive Vajradhara, Lord of an ocean of mandalas and lineages, endowed with the meaning of the supreme symbols, incomparably kind, great Spiritual Guide, Kelsang Gyatso Rinpoche, may we offer in your presence a requesting mandala beseeching you to remain with a lifespan of a hundred thousand aeons for the sake of the doctrine and migrators.

Now everyone recites:

OM VAJRA BHUMI AH HUM
Great and powerful golden ground,
OM VAJRA REKHE AH HUM
At the edge the iron fence stands around the outer circle.
In the centre Mount Meru the king of mountains,
Around which are four continents:
In the east, Purvavideha, in the south, Jambudipa,
In the west, Aparagodaniya, in the north, Uttarakuru.
Each has two sub-continents:
Deha and Videha, Tsamara and Abatsamara,

Satha and Uttaramantrina, Kurava and Kaurava.
The mountain of jewels, the wish-granting tree,
The wish-granting cow, and the harvest unsown.
The precious wheel, the precious jewel,
The precious queen, the precious minister,
The precious elephant, the precious supreme horse,
The precious general, and the great treasure vase.
The goddess of beauty, the goddess of garlands,
The goddess of song, the goddess of dance,
The goddess of flowers, the goddess of incense,
The goddess of light, and the goddess of scent.
The sun and the moon, the precious umbrella,
The banner of victory in every direction.
In the centre all treasures of both gods and men,
An excellent collection with nothing left out.
We offer this to you our kind root Guru and lineage
    Gurus,
And especially to you, Lord of an ocean of mandalas and
    lineages,
Endowed with the meaning of the supreme symbols,
Incomparably kind, great Spiritual Guide, Kelsang Gyatso
    Rinpoche,
We offer in your presence a requesting mandala beseeching
    you to remain with a life span of a hundred thousand
    aeons for the sake of the doctrine and migrators.
Please accept with compassion for migrating beings,
And having accepted, out of your great compassion,
Please bestow your blessings on all sentient beings
    pervading space.

The ground sprinkled with perfume and spread with
    flowers,
The Great Mountain, four lands, sun and moon,
Seen as a Buddha Land and offered thus,
May all beings enjoy such Pure Lands.

In the space before me on a lion throne, lotus and moon
The venerable Gurus smile with delight.
O Supreme Field of Merit for our minds of faith,
Please remain for a hundred aeons to spread the doctrine.

O Losang, Principal Buddha, Vajradhara,
Please reveal your all-pervasive outer, inner and secret
    bodies,
And with a compassionate intention towards migrators as
    extensive as space,
Please turn the outer, inner and secret Dharma Wheels.

IDAM GURU RATNA MANDALAKAM NIRYATAYAMI

Return to page 217.

Appendix IX:
The Hundreds of Deities of the Joyful Land According to Highest Yoga Tantra

THE GURU YOGA OF JE TSONGKHAPA AS A PRELIMINARY PRACTICE FOR MAHAMUDRA

Here, 'Guru' is the Spiritual Guide who leads us to the correct spiritual path and who shows a good example. Through following the correct spiritual path we can accomplish all our temporary and ultimate aims. In this context, 'yoga' means a ritual practice that is a special way of relying upon the Spiritual Guide. Since the root of all spiritual realizations of Sutra and Tantra is relying purely upon the Spiritual Guide, the practice of Guru yoga is an essential practice of Buddhism.

For many people reciting prayers out loud makes it difficult to concentrate on the meaning, because the sound interferes with their concentration. Therefore we need to become familiar with reciting mentally from our heart without sound, which means that we need to memorize our daily prayers.

Dorjechang Kelsang Gyatso Rinpoche

HOW TO PRACTISE THIS GURU YOGA

Visualization

In the space before me appears my root Guru, Guru Sumati Buddha Heruka, surrounded by all the Buddhas of the ten directions.

We recite this while contemplating the meaning, and then briefly meditate with strong faith on the assembly of the objects of refuge and the commitment beings of the Field of Merit.

Taking the Mahayana refuge vows

O Gurus, Buddhas and Bodhisattvas, please listen to me.
I and all mother living beings as extensive as space
From now until we attain enlightenment
Go for refuge to the Three Precious Jewels – Buddha,
 Dharma and Sangha.

(3x)

We recite this three times and make a strong promise, 'From now until I attain enlightenment I will rely upon and hold only Buddha, Dharma and Sangha as my ultimate refuge.' In this way we take the Mahayana refuge vows.

Taking the Bodhisattva vow according to Highest Yoga Tantra

For the sake of all mother sentient beings,
I shall become the Guru-Deity,
And then lead every sentient being
To the Guru-Deity's supreme state.

(3x)

We recite this three times while contemplating its meaning and make this promise sincerely. In this way we generate bodhichitta and take the Bodhisattva vow according to Highest Yoga Tantra.

Inviting the wisdom beings

From the heart of the Protector of the hundreds of Deities of the Joyful Land,
To the peak of a cloud, which is like a cluster of fresh, white curd,
All-knowing Losang Dragpa, King of the Dharma,
Please come to this place together with your Sons.

Reciting this we contemplate that from the sphere of the infinite space of bliss and emptiness at the heart of Protector Buddha Maitreya abiding in the Pure Land of the Joyful Land we invite the wisdom beings, King of the Dharma All-knowing Je Tsongkhapa surrounded by the Buddhas of the ten directions. They all dissolve into the commitment beings in the space in front and we think that the wisdom beings and commitment beings become inseparably one.

Requesting

In the space before me on a lion throne, lotus and moon,
The venerable Gurus smile with delight.
O Supreme Field of Merit for my mind of faith,
Please remain for a hundred aeons to spread the doctrine.

> *Reciting this we make the request, 'O Venerable Spiritual
> Guide, wherever I may be, please appear in the space before
> me and with delight remain for a hundred thousand aeons
> as a field in which I can sow the seeds of faith, and the
> object through whom I can accumulate the collection of
> merit.'*

The seven limbs

Prostration

Your mind of wisdom realizes the full extent of objects of
    knowledge,
Your eloquent speech is the ear-ornament of the fortunate,
Your beautiful body is ablaze with the glory of renown,
I prostrate to you, whom to see, to hear and to remember is
    so meaningful.

> *Reciting this we strongly believe that we are prostrating
> to countless objects of refuge for countless aeons, with
> countless bodies that we have emanated through the force
> of correct imagination, while remembering their kindness
> and good qualities.*

Offering

Pleasing water offerings, various flowers,
Sweet-smelling incense, lights, scented water and so forth,
A vast cloud of offerings both set out and imagined,
I offer to you, O Supreme Field of Merit.

*We contemplate and believe that all worlds are completely
pure Buddha Lands with masses of outer, inner and secret
offerings generated through the force of concentration –
inconceivable clouds of completely pure offerings covering
all the ground and filling the whole of space – and we
imagine making these offerings for countless aeons to the
supreme Field of Merit, the assembly of Deities of Guru
Sumati Buddha Heruka.*

Purification

Whatever non-virtues of body, speech and mind
I have accumulated since time without beginning,
Especially transgressions of my three vows,
With great remorse I confess each one from the depths
   of my heart.

*We cry out to Guru Sumati Buddha Heruka, 'All the
negativities, downfalls and broken commitments I have
accumulated with my body, speech and mind, throughout
all my countless lives until now, I confess with a mind of
strong regret and strong promise. O Protector, through the
power of your compassion please bless me to purify them
now.' We contemplate this again and again from the very
depths of our heart to make purification.*

Rejoicing

In this degenerate age you strove for much learning and
accomplishment.
Abandoning the eight worldly concerns, you made your
freedom and endowment meaningful.
O Protector, from the very depths of my heart,
I rejoice in the great wave of your deeds.

*We promise, 'O Venerable Guru, I rejoice from the depths
of my heart in your skilful deeds through which you lead
so many fortunate beings to the state of the Union of
enlightenment, and I promise to become just like you.'*

Requesting the turning of the Wheel of Dharma

From the billowing clouds of wisdom and compassion
In the space of your Truth Body, O Venerable and holy
Gurus,
Please send down a rain of vast and profound Dharma
Appropriate to the disciples of this world.

*We request, 'O Venerable Guru, from the billowing clouds
of wisdom and compassion in the space of your Truth Body,
Dharmakaya, please emanate countless different Spiritual
Guides pervading the whole world according to the needs
of disciples, and pour down a rain of vast and profound
Dharma of the Ganden Oral Lineage upon countless
disciples.'*

Beseeching the Spiritual Guides not to pass away

From your actual deathless body, born from meaning clear
　　light,
Please send countless emanations throughout the world
To spread the Oral Lineage of the Ganden doctrine;
And may they remain for a very long time.

> *We make the single-pointed request, 'O Protector, although
> your body of Union arisen from meaning clear light has no
> death, the various kinds of Spiritual Guide you emanate
> as ordinary beings are not deathless. We request these
> Spiritual Guides never to pass away but to remain until
> samsara ends.'*

Dedication

Through the virtues I have accumulated here,
May the doctrine and all living beings receive every benefit.
Especially may the essence of the doctrine
Of Venerable Losang Dragpa shine forever.

> *We dedicate all the virtues we and others have accumulated
> up to now to benefit the doctrine and all living beings, and
> especially for the essence of Je Tsongkhapa's doctrine, the
> instructions and practice of the Ganden Oral Lineage, to
> increase and spread throughout the entire world.*

Offering the mandala

> *We make either a long or short mandala offering to Guru
> Sumati Buddha Heruka together with his assembly of
> Deities.*

OM VAJRA BHUMI AH HUM
Great and powerful golden ground,
OM VAJRA REKHE AH HUM
At the edge the iron fence stands around the outer circle.
In the centre Mount Meru the king of mountains,
Around which are four continents:
In the east, Purvavideha, in the south, Jambudipa,
In the west, Aparagodaniya, in the north, Uttarakuru.
Each has two sub-continents:
Deha and Videha, Tsamara and Abatsamara,
Satha and Uttaramantrina, Kurava and Kaurava.
The mountain of jewels, the wish-granting tree,
The wish-granting cow, and the harvest unsown.
The precious wheel, the precious jewel,
The precious queen, the precious minister,
The precious elephant, the precious supreme horse,
The precious general, and the great treasure vase.
The goddess of beauty, the goddess of garlands,
The goddess of song, the goddess of dance,
The goddess of flowers, the goddess of incense,
The goddess of light, and the goddess of scent.
The sun and the moon, the precious umbrella,
The banner of victory in every direction.
In the centre all treasures of both gods and men,
An excellent collection with nothing left out.
I offer this to you my kind root Guru and lineage Gurus,
To all of you sacred and glorious Gurus,
And especially to you, Guru Sumati Buddha Heruka
together with your retinues.
Please accept with compassion for migrating beings,

And having accepted, out of your great compassion,
Please bestow your blessings on all sentient beings
    pervading space.

The ground sprinkled with perfume and spread with
    flowers,
The Great Mountain, four lands, sun and moon,
Seen as a Buddha Land and offered thus,
May all beings enjoy such Pure Lands.

I offer without any sense of loss
The objects that give rise to my attachment, hatred and
    confusion,
My friends, enemies and strangers, our bodies and
    enjoyments;
Please accept these and bless me to be released directly
    from the three poisons.

IDAM GURU RATNA MANDALAKAM NIRYATAYAMI

> *We make this mandala offering with strong faith,
> transforming the entire universe into a Pure Land of
> Buddha through correct imagination, and offer this Pure
> Land of Buddha to the assembly of Deities of Guru Sumati
> Buddha Heruka together with their retinues.*

Reciting the *Migtsema* request prayer according to Highest Yoga Tantra

O Guru Sumati Buddha Heruka, synthesis of all three
    lineages in one,
I request you, please dispel all my outer and inner
    obstacles,

Ripen my mental continuum, liberate me from dualistic
   appearance,
And bless me so that I will effortlessly benefit all living
   beings.

*In this context 'three lineages' refers to the body, speech
and mind of all Buddhas.*

   *We recite this Migtsema request prayer seven or more
times.*

   *Traditionally in this practice we need to collect at least
a hundred thousand of this Migtsema request prayer
with strong faith and while contemplating its meaning.
Through this we will receive powerful blessings.*

Request to the Lord of All Lineages
*Request prayer for the practice of Lamrim, Lojong,
generation stage and completion stage*

*Being completely free from distractions, we should
concentrate on the meaning of the following words.*

   *We make a strong request and encourage ourself to
practise each and every stage of the paths of Sutra and
Tantra, and make a strong determination to accomplish
the actual realization of each and every one.*

   *We should practise like this every day; there is no greater
meaning than this. Please keep this advice in your heart.*

O Venerable Conqueror Losang Dragpa,
Who are the Glorious Lord of all lineages, Heruka,
In whose single body all Buddhas, their worlds and their
   retinues abide,
I request you please bestow your blessings.

My kind, precious root Guru,
Who are inseparably one with Heruka,
In whose great bliss all phenomena are gathered into one,
I request you please bestow your blessings.

Since the root of all spiritual attainments
Is relying purely upon the Spiritual Guide,
Please now bestow the profound blessings of your body,
    speech and mind
Upon my body, speech and mind.

Out of his great kindness Je Tsongkhapa introduced
All the Sutra and Tantra teachings of Buddha as practical
    instructions.
However, my great good fortune in having met holy
    Dharma, the doctrine of Buddha,
Might remain with me for just this one life.

Yet my breath is like mist about to vanish
And my life is like a candle flame about to die in the wind.
Since there is no guarantee I will not die today,
Now is the only time to take the real meaning of human
    life, the attainment of enlightenment.

In my countless former lives I accumulated various kinds
    of non-virtuous action
And as a result I will have to experience the unbearable
    suffering of lower rebirth for many aeons.
Since this is unbearable for me, I sincerely seek refuge
In Buddha, Dharma and Sangha from the depths of my
    heart.

I will sincerely apply effort
To receiving Buddha's blessings,
Receiving help from Sangha, the pure spiritual
    practitioners,
And practising Dharma purely.

Through engaging in this practice continuously
I will accomplish the actual refuge in my mind –
The realizations of holy Dharma
That permanently liberate me from all suffering and
    problems.

The cause of suffering is non-virtuous actions
And the cause of happiness is virtuous actions.
Since this is completely true
I will definitely abandon the first and practise the second.

Like mistakenly believing
A poisonous drink to be nectar,
Attachment with grasping at objects of desire
Is the cause of great danger.

In the cycle of impure life, samsara,
There is no real protection from suffering.
Wherever I am born, either as a lower or higher being,
I will have to experience only suffering.

The flesh and bones of all the bodies I have previously
    taken if gathered together would be equal to Mount
    Meru,
And if the blood and bodily fluids were gathered they
    would be equal to the deepest ocean.

Although I have taken countless bodies as Brahma, Indra,
    chakravatin kings, gods and ordinary humans,
There has been no meaning from any of these, for still I
    continue to suffer.

If having been born in the hells drinking molten copper, as
    insects whose bodies turned into mud,
And as dogs, pigs and so forth who ate enough filth to
    cover the whole earth,
And if, as it is said, the tears I have shed from all this
    suffering are vaster than an ocean,
I still do not feel any sorrow or fear, do I have a mind made
    of iron?

Understanding this, I will make continuous effort to cease
    samsaric rebirth
By striving to permanently abandon its root, self-grasping
    ignorance.
In dependence upon this renunciation I will open the door
    to the path to liberation
And strive to practise the three higher trainings, the
    synthesis of all paths.

With my mind like a fine horse heading for higher ground
Guided by the reins of the Dharma of the three higher
    trainings,
And urged onwards with the whip of strong effort,
Now I will swiftly travel the path to liberation.

All mother living beings who care for me with such
    kindness
Are drowning in the fearful ocean of samsara.

If I give no thought to their pitiful suffering
I am like a mean and heartless child.

Since throughout my beginningless lives until now, the root
of all my suffering has been my self-cherishing mind,
I must expel it from my heart, cast it afar and cherish only
other living beings.
Thus, I will complete my practice of exchanging self with
others.
O my precious Guru, please bestow your blessings so that I
may complete this profound practice.

To permanently liberate all mother living beings
From suffering and mistaken appearance,
I will attain the Union of the state of enlightenment
Through the practice of the six perfections.

Eliminating the distractions of my mind completely,
Observing and holding a single object of meditation with
mindfulness,
And preventing the obstacles of mental sinking and mental
excitement from arising,
In this way I will control my mind with clear and joyful
meditation.

All my appearances in dreams teach me
That all my appearances when awake do not exist;
Thus for me all my dream appearances
Are the supreme instructions of my Guru.

The phenomena that I normally see or perceive
Are deceptive – created by mistaken minds.

If I search for the reality of what I see,
There is nothing there that exists – I perceive only empty
　　like space.

When I search with my wisdom eye,
All the things that I normally see disappear
And only their mere name remains.
With this mere name I simply accept everything for the
　　purpose of communicating with others.

The way phenomena exist is just this.
Guru Father Je Tsongkhapa clarified this following
　　Nagarjuna's intention.
Thus, the correct view of emptiness free from the two
　　extremes
Is extremely profound.

With my having experience of the common paths,
The principal of Akanishta Pure Land, Vajradhara Heruka,
Now appears in this world as an emanation of Heruka
In the form of my root Guru
Who has led me inside the great mandala of the body of
　　Heruka
And granted me the four empowerments to ripen my
　　mental continuum.
Thus I have become a great fortunate one who has the
　　opportunity to accomplish in this life
The Union of Heruka by accomplishing No More Learning,
　　the state of enlightenment.

The kindness of Guru Heruka Father and Mother is
　　inconceivable

And the kindness of my root Guru is inconceivable.
Because of this good fortune and through the power of my
correct imagination
I now abide in the great mandala of Heruka, the nature of
my purified gross body.

I am the enlightened Deity Heruka,
The nature of my purified white indestructible drop,
With my consort Vajravarahi,
The nature of my purified red indestructible drop.
I am surrounded by the Bodhisattva Deities, the Heroes
and Heroines,
Who are the nature of my purified channels and drops.
Through enjoying great bliss and the emptiness of all
phenomena I have pacified all ordinary appearances and
conceptions,
And thus I have accomplished the real meaning of human
life.

Having generated myself as Heruka with consort,
I meditate briefly on my body as hollow and empty like
space.
Within this body is my central channel possessing four
characteristics.
Inside my central channel in the centre of the eight petals of
the heart channel wheel
Is the union of my white and red indestructible drop, the
size of a small pea,
Which is very clear and radiates five-coloured lights.
Inside this is my indestructible wind in the aspect of a letter
HUM,

Which is actual Glorious Heruka.
My mind enters into the HUM and mixes with it like
water mixing with water.
I hold this HUM, which is my indestructible wind
and Heruka, with mindfulness and meditate on it
single-pointedly.

Through stabilizing this meditation the movement of my
inner winds of conceptions will cease.
Thus, I will perceive a fully qualified clear light.
Through completing the practice of this clear light
I will attain the actual Union of Great Keajra, the state of
enlightenment.
This is the great kindness of Guru Heruka;
May I become just like you.

Receiving blessings

O Glorious and precious root Guru,
Please sit on the lotus and moon seat at my heart.
Please care for me with your great kindness,
And grant me the blessings of your body, speech and mind.

*As a result of this request, all the Buddhas of the ten
directions in the space in front melt into light and dissolve
into Venerable Guru Tsongkhapa. He in turn melts into
light and dissolves into Buddha Shakyamuni at his heart.
Then Buddha Shakyamuni melts into light and dissolves
into Heruka at his heart.*

*With great delight, Guru Heruka comes to my crown and
abides in the central channel in the centre of my crown*

channel wheel. Lights radiate from his body and bless the
channels, winds and drops at my crown.

O Glorious and precious root Guru,
Please sit on the lotus and moon seat at my heart.
Please care for me with your great kindness,
And bestow the common and supreme attainments.

As a result of this request, Guru Heruka comes to my
throat and abides in the central channel in the centre of
my throat channel wheel. Lights radiate from his body and
bless the channels, winds and drops at my throat.

O Glorious and precious root Guru,
Please sit on the lotus and moon seat at my heart.
Please care for me with your great kindness,
And remain firm until I attain the essence of enlightenment.

As a result of this request, Guru Heruka comes to my heart
and abides in the central channel in the centre of my heart
channel wheel. Lights radiate from his body and bless the
channels, winds and drops at my heart.

Then Guru Heruka's mind of clear light of great bliss mixes
with my mind and they become non-dual, of one nature.
Through the force of this, my mind becomes the nature of
Heruka's mind of clear light of great bliss.

We meditate briefly on our mind, which is the clear light
of great bliss of Heruka's mind accomplished through the
force of correct imagination, and hold it single-pointedly
without forgetting it.

Then with a feeling of great joy we engage in the actual practice of Mahamudra by practising the following as explained in the book The Oral Instructions of Mahamudra:

1. *Having identified our own mind, meditating on tranquil abiding*
2. *Having realized emptiness, meditating on superior seeing*
3. *Meditating on the central channel, the yoga of the central channel*
4. *Meditating on the indestructible drop, the yoga of the drop*
5. *Meditating on the indestructible wind, the yoga of wind*

Dedication

Through being cared for throughout all my lives
By Conqueror Tsongkhapa as my Mahayana Guru,
May I never turn away, even for an instant,
From this excellent path praised by the Conquerors.

Through the practices of pure moral discipline, extensive
    listening,
Training in bodhichitta, pure view, pure conduct and
    so forth,
May I and all living beings sincerely practise purely
    and unmistakenly
The doctrine of Conqueror Losang Dragpa.

Prayer for the Virtuous Tradition

So that the tradition of Je Tsongkhapa,
The King of the Dharma, may flourish,
May all obstacles be pacified
And may all favourable conditions abound.

Through the two collections of myself and others
Gathered throughout the three times,
May the doctrine of Conqueror Losang Dragpa
Flourish for evermore.

The nine-line *Migtsema* prayer

Tsongkhapa, crown ornament of the scholars of the Land
    of the Snows,
You are Buddha Shakyamuni and Vajradhara, the source
    of all attainments,
Avalokiteshvara, the treasury of unobservable compassion,
Manjushri, the supreme stainless wisdom,
And Vajrapani, the destroyer of the hosts of maras.
O Venerable Guru-Buddha, synthesis of all Three Jewels,
With my body, speech and mind, respectfully I make
    requests:
Please grant your blessings to ripen and liberate myself
    and others,
And bestow the common and supreme attainments.

(3x)

Colophon: This sadhana or ritual prayer for spiritual attainments
was compiled by Venerable Geshe Kelsang Gyatso Rinpoche
from traditional sources, 2015.

Glossary

Amitabha   The manifestation of the speech of all Buddhas, and of their aggregate of discrimination. He has a red-coloured body. See *The New Eight Steps to Happiness*.

Anger   A deluded mental factor that observes its contaminated object, exaggerates its bad qualities, considers it to be undesirable, and wishes to harm it. See *How to Understand the Mind* and *How to Solve Our Human Problems*.

Aryadeva   A third century AD Indian Buddhist scholar and meditation master, who was a disciple of Nagarjuna.

Atisha   (AD 982-1054) A famous Indian Buddhist scholar and meditation master. He was Abbot of the great Buddhist monastery of Vikramashila at a time when Mahayana Buddhism was flourishing in India. He was later invited to Tibet where he re-introduced pure Buddhism. He is the author of the first text on the stages of the path, *Lamp for the Path*. His tradition later became known as the 'Kadampa Tradition'. See *Joyful Path of Good Fortune* and *Modern Buddhism*.

Attachment   A deluded mental factor that observes its contaminated object, regards it as a cause of happiness and wishes for it. See *How to Understand the Mind*.

Attainment   'Siddhi' in Sanskrit. These are of two types: common attainments and supreme attainments. Common attainments are of four principal types: pacifying attainments (the ability to purify negativity, overcome obstacles and cure

273

sickness), increasing attainments (the ability to increase Dharma realizations, merit, lifespan and wealth), controlling attainments (the ability to control one's own and others' minds and actions) and wrathful attainments (the ability to use wrathful actions where appropriate to benefit others). Supreme attainments are the special realizations of a Buddha. See *Tantric Grounds and Paths*.

Blessing   The transformation of our mind from a negative state to a positive state, from an unhappy state to a happy state, or from a state of weakness to a state of strength, through the inspiration of holy beings such as our Spiritual Guide, Buddhas and Bodhisattvas.

Bodhisattva   A person who has generated spontaneous bodhichitta but who has not yet become a Buddha. From the moment a practitioner generates a non-artificial, or spontaneous, bodhichitta, he or she becomes a Bodhisattva and enters the first Mahayana path, the path of accumulation. An ordinary Bodhisattva is one who has not realized emptiness directly, and a Superior Bodhisattva is one who has attained a direct realization of emptiness. See *Joyful Path of Good Fortune* and *Meaningful to Behold*.

Body mandala   The transformation into a Deity of any part of the body of a self-generated or in-front-generated Deity. See *Essence of Vajrayana*, *The New Guide to Dakini Land* and *Great Treasury of Merit*.

Buddha's bodies   A Buddha has four bodies – the Wisdom Truth Body, the Nature Body, the Enjoyment Body, and the Emanation Body. The first is Buddha's omniscient mind. The second is the emptiness, or ultimate nature, of his or her mind. The third is his subtle Form Body. The fourth, of which each Buddha manifests a countless number, are gross Form Bodies that are visible to ordinary beings. The Wisdom Truth Body and the Nature Body are both included within the Truth Body, and the Enjoyment Body and the Emanation Body are both included within the Form Body. See *Joyful Path of Good Fortune* and *Ocean of Nectar*.

Buddha nature   The root mind of a living being, and its ultimate nature. Buddha nature, Buddha seed, and Buddha lineage are synonyms. All living beings have Buddha nature and therefore the potential to attain Buddhahood. See *Mahamudra Tantra*.

Buddha Shakyamuni   The fourth of one thousand founding Buddhas who are to appear in this world during this Fortunate Aeon. The first three were Krakuchchanda, Kanakamuni and Kashyapa. The fifth Buddha will be Maitreya.

Central channel   The principal channel at the very centre of the body, along which the channel wheels are located. See *Clear Light of Bliss*, *Mahamudra Tantra* and *Modern Buddhism*.

'Chod' or 'cutting' practice   A ritual practice, combining compassion and wisdom, for destroying self-cherishing and self-grasping through correctly imagining cutting up our body, and giving this to spirits and offering it to holy beings.

Clear light   A manifest very subtle mind that perceives an appearance like clear, empty space. See *Clear Light of Bliss*, *Mahamudra Tantra* and *Modern Buddhism*.

Collection of merit   A virtuous action motivated by bodhichitta that is a main cause of attaining the Form Body of a Buddha. Examples are: making offerings and prostrations to holy beings with bodhichitta motivation, and the practice of the perfections of giving, moral discipline, and patience.

Collection of wisdom   A virtuous mental action motivated by bodhichitta that is a main cause of attaining the Truth Body of a Buddha. Examples are: listening to, contemplating and meditating on emptiness with bodhichitta motivation.

Completion stage   Highest Yoga Tantra realizations developed in dependence upon the winds entering, abiding and dissolving within the central channel through the force of meditation. See *Clear Light of Bliss*, *Mahamudra Tantra*, *Tantric Grounds and Paths*, *The New Guide to Dakini Land* and *Essence of Vajrayana*.

Compositional factors   The aggregate of compositional factors comprises all mental factors except feeling and discrimination, as well as non-associated compounded phenomena. See *The New Heart of Wisdom* and *How to Understand the Mind*.

Dakini Land   The Pure Land of Heruka and Vajrayogini. In Sanskrit it is called 'Keajra' and in Tibetan 'Dagpa Khacho'. See *The New Guide to Dakini Land*.

Dedication   Dedication is by nature a virtuous mental factor; it is the virtuous intention that functions both to prevent accumulated virtue from degenerating and to cause its increase. See *Joyful Path of Good Fortune*.

Deluded view   A view that functions to obstruct the attainment of liberation. See *How to Understand the Mind*.

Delusion   A mental factor that arises from inappropriate attention and functions to make the mind unpeaceful and uncontrolled. There are three main delusions: ignorance, desirous attachment and anger. From these arise all the other delusions, such as jealousy, pride and deluded doubt. See *Joyful Path of Good Fortune* and *How to Understand the Mind*.

Demi-god   A being of the demi-god realm, the second highest of the six realms of samsara. Demi-gods are similar to gods but their bodies, possessions, and environments are inferior. See *Joyful Path of Good Fortune*.

Desire realm   The environment of hell beings, hungry spirits, animals, human beings, demi-gods, and the gods who enjoy the five objects of desire.

Dharmavajra   (born AD 1457) A great Tibetan Mahasiddha and Mahamudra lineage Guru.

Discrimination   A mental factor that functions to apprehend the uncommon sign of an object. See *How to Understand the Mind*.

Distraction   A deluded mental factor that wanders to any object of delusion. See *How to Understand the Mind*.

Emanation Body   See *Buddha's bodies*.

Empowerment   The gateway through which we enter Tantra is receiving a Tantric empowerment, which bestows upon us special blessings that heal our mental continuum and awaken our Buddha nature. When we receive a Tantric empowerment, we are sowing the special seeds of the four bodies of a Buddha upon our mental continuum. See *Mahamudra Tantra* and *Tantric Grounds and Paths*.

Enjoyment Body   See *Buddha's bodies*.

Faith   A naturally virtuous mind that functions mainly to oppose the perception of faults in its observed object. There are three types of faith: believing faith, admiring faith and wishing faith. See *Modern Buddhism*, *How to Transform Your Life* and *How to Understand the Mind*.

Feeling   A mental factor that functions to experience pleasant, unpleasant or neutral objects. See *How to Understand the Mind*.

Form Body   The Enjoyment Body and the Emanation Body of a Buddha. See also *Buddha's bodies*. See *Joyful Path of Good Fortune*.

Ganden   'Tushita' in Sanskrit, 'Joyful Land' in English. The Pure Land of Buddha Maitreya. Both Je Tsongkhapa and Atisha went to this Pure Land after they passed away. Also the name of the monastery in Tibet founded by Je Tsongkhapa, and of the special doctrine revealed by Je Tsongkhapa. See *Heart Jewel*.

Ganden Emanation Scripture   Also known as *Kadam Emanation Scripture*. A special scripture, the nature of Manjushri's wisdom, revealed directly to Je Tsongkhapa by Manjushri. It contains instructions on Vajrayana Mahamudra, *Offering to the Spiritual Guide* (*Lama Chopa*), *The Hundreds of Deities of the Joyful Land* (*Ganden Lhagyema*), the *Migtsema* prayer, and six sadhanas of Manjushri. This scripture was not composed in ordinary letters, and only highly realized beings can consult it directly. At first the instructions from this scripture were passed down only by word of mouth from Teacher to disciple, and so the lineage became known as the 'Uncommon Whispered Lineage of the Virtuous Tradition' or the 'Ensa Whispered Lineage'. It is also known as the 'Uncommon Close Lineage' because it was revealed directly to Je Tsongkhapa by Manjushri. Later, scholars such as the first Panchen Lama (AD 1569-1662) wrote down the instructions from this scripture in ordinary letters. See *Great Treasury of Merit* and *Heart Jewel*.

Generation stage   A realization of a creative yoga prior to attaining the actual completion stage, which is attained through the practice of bringing the three bodies into the path, in which one mentally generates oneself as a Tantric Deity and one's surroundings as the Deity's mandala. Meditation on generation stage is called a 'creative yoga' because its object is created, or generated, by correct imagination. See *Tantric Grounds and Paths*, *Mahamudra Tantra*, *The New Guide to Dakini Land*, and *Essence of Vajrayana*.

Geshe   A title given by Kadampa monasteries to accomplished Buddhist scholars. Contracted form of the Tibetan 'ge wai she nyen', literally meaning 'virtuous friend'.

God   'Deva' in Sanskrit. Beings of the god realm, the highest of the six realms of samsara. There are many different types of god. Some are desire realm gods, while others are form or formless realm gods. See *Joyful Path of Good Fortune*.

Gungtang   Gungtang Konchog Tenpai Dronme (AD 1762-1823), a Gelug scholar and meditator famous for his spiritual poems and philosophical writings.

Gyalwa Ensapa   (AD 1505-1566) A great Yogi and Mahamudra lineage Guru who attained enlightenment in three years. See *Great Treasury of Merit*.

Happiness   There are two types of happiness: mundane and supramundane. Mundane happiness is the limited happiness that can be found within samsara, such as the happiness of human beings and gods. Supramundane happiness is the pure happiness of liberation and enlightenment.

Heart Sutra   One of several *Perfection of Wisdom Sutras* taught by Buddha. Although much shorter than the other *Perfection of Wisdom Sutras*, it contains explicitly or implicitly their entire meaning. Also known as the *Essence of Wisdom Sutra*. For a translation and full commentary, see *The New Heart of Wisdom*.

Hell beings   Beings of the hell realm, the lowest of the six realms of samsara. See *Joyful Path of Good Fortune*.

Heroines and Heroes   A Heroine is a female Tantric Deity embodying wisdom. A Hero is a male Tantric Deity embodying method. See *The New Guide to Dakini Land*.

Highest Yoga Tantra   The supreme quick path to enlightenment. The teachings on Highest Yoga Tantra are Buddha's ultimate intention. See also *Tantra*. See *Mahamudra Tantra* and *Tantric Grounds and Paths*.

Hinayana   Sanskrit term for 'Lesser Vehicle'. The Hinayana goal is to attain merely one's own liberation from suffering by completely abandoning delusions. See *Joyful Path of Good Fortune*.

Hundreds of Deities of the Joyful Land   *Ganden Lhagyema* in Tibetan. A special Guru yoga of Je Tsongkhapa in which Je Tsongkhapa and his two Sons are invited from the Joyful Land, or Tushita. This is incorporated into a number of sadhana practices, including *The Hundreds of Deities of the Joyful Land According to Highest Yoga Tantra*, see page 251. See also the book *Heart Jewel*.

Hungry ghosts   Beings of the hungry ghost realm, the second lowest of the six realms of samsara. Also known as 'hungry spirits'. See *Joyful Path of Good Fortune*.

Illusory body   The subtle divine body that is principally developed from the indestructible wind. When a practitioner of Highest Yoga Tantra rises from the meditation of the isolated mind of ultimate example clear light, he or she attains a body that is not the same as his or her ordinary physical body. This new body is the illusory body. It has the same appearance as the body of the personal Deity of generation stage except that it is white in colour. It can be perceived only by those who have already attained an illusory body. See *Clear Light of Bliss* and *Tantric Grounds and Paths*.

Imprint   There are two types of imprint: imprints of actions and imprints of delusions. Every action we perform leaves an imprint on the mental consciousness, and these imprints are karmic potentialities to experience certain effects in the future. The imprints left by delusions remain even after the delusions themselves have been abandoned, rather as the smell of garlic lingers in a container after the garlic has been removed. Imprints of delusions are obstructions to omniscience, and are completely abandoned only by Buddhas.

Intermediate state   'Bardo' in Tibetan. The state between death and rebirth. It begins the moment the consciousness leaves the body, and ceases the moment the consciousness enters the body of the next life. See *Joyful Path of Good Fortune* and *Clear Light of Bliss*.

Je Phabongkhapa   (AD 1878-1941) A great Tibetan Lama who was an emanation of Heruka. Phabongkha Rinpoche was the holder of many lineages of Sutra and Secret Mantra. He was the root Guru of Vajradhara Trijang Rinpoche.

Kadampa A Tibetan word in which 'Ka' means 'word' and refers to all Buddha's teachings, 'dam' refers to Atisha's special Lamrim instructions known as the 'stages of the path to enlightenment', and 'pa' refers to a follower of Kadampa Buddhism who integrates all the teachings of Buddha that they know into their Lamrim practice. See also *Kadampa Buddhism*.

Kadampa Buddhism A Mahayana Buddhist school founded by the great Indian Buddhist Master Atisha (AD 982-1054). See also *Kadampa*. See *Modern Buddhism*.

Lama Losang Tubwang Dorjechang A special manifestation of Je Tsongkhapa revealed directly to the great Yogi Dharmavajra. In this manifestation, Je Tsongkhapa appears as a fully ordained monk wearing a long-eared Pandit's hat, with Buddha Shakyamuni at his heart, and Conqueror Vajradhara at his heart. In the practice of *Offering to the Spiritual Guide*, we visualize our Spiritual Guide in this aspect. 'Lama' indicates that he is our Spiritual Guide, 'Losang' that he is Je Tsongkhapa (whose ordained name was Losang Dragpa), 'Tubwang' that he is Buddha Shakyamuni, and 'Dorjechang' that he is Vajradhara. In Tibetan, this aspect of our Spiritual Guide is also known as 'je sempa sum tseg', which means 'Je Tsongkhapa, the Unification of Three Holy Beings'. This indicates that in reality our Spiritual Guide is the same nature as Je Tsongkhapa, Buddha Shakyamuni, and Conqueror Vajradhara. See *Great Treasury of Merit*.

Lamrim A Tibetan term, literally meaning 'stages of the path'. A special arrangement of all Buddha's teachings that is easy to understand and put into practice. It reveals all the stages of the path to enlightenment. For a full commentary, see *Joyful Path of Good Fortune* and *The New Meditation Handbook*.

Laziness A deluded mental factor that, motivated by attachment to worldly pleasures or worldly activities, dislikes virtuous activity. There are three types of laziness: laziness arising from attachment to worldly pleasures, laziness arising from attachment to distracting activities, and laziness arising from discouragement. See *Joyful Path of Good Fortune* and *How to Understand the Mind*.

Living being Any being who possesses a mind that is contaminated by delusions or their imprints. Both 'living being' and 'sentient being' are terms used to distinguish beings whose minds are contaminated by either of these two obstructions from Buddhas, whose minds are completely free from these obstructions.

Mahamudra A Sanskrit term, literally meaning 'great seal'. According to Sutra, this refers to the profound view of emptiness. Since emptiness is the nature of all phenomena, it is called a 'seal', and since a direct realization of emptiness enables us to accomplish the great purpose – complete liberation from the sufferings of samsara – it is also called 'great'. According to Tantra, or Vajrayana, great seal is the union of spontaneous great bliss and emptiness. See *The Oral Instructions of Mahamudra*, *Mahamudra Tantra*, *Great Treasury of Merit* and *Clear Light of Bliss*.

Mahayana Sanskrit term for 'Great Vehicle', the spiritual path to great enlightenment. The Mahayana goal is to attain Buddhahood for the benefit of all sentient beings by completely abandoning delusions and their imprints. See *Joyful Path of Good Fortune* and *Meaningful to Behold*.

Mala A set of prayer beads used to count recitations of prayers or mantras, usually with one hundred and eight beads. See *The New Guide to Dakini Land*.

Mandala offering An offering of the entire universe visualized as a Pure Land, with all its inhabitants as pure beings. See *The New Guide to Dakini Land* and *Great Treasury of Merit*.

Mantra   A Sanskrit word, literally meaning 'mind protection'. Mantra protects the mind from ordinary appearances and conceptions. There are four types of mantra: mantras that are mind, mantras that are inner wind, mantras that are sound, and mantras that are form. In general, there are three types of mantra recitation: verbal recitation, mental recitation and vajra recitation. See *Modern Buddhism* and *Tantric Grounds and Paths*.

Meaning clear light   A mind of clear light that realizes emptiness directly without a generic image. Synonymous with inner Dakini Land. See *Clear Light of Bliss* and *Tantric Grounds and Paths*.

Mental factor   A cognizer that principally apprehends a particular attribute of an object. There are fifty-one specific mental factors. Each moment of mind comprises a primary mind and various mental factors. See *How to Understand the Mind*.

Merit   The good fortune created by virtuous actions. It is the potential power to increase our good qualities and produce happiness.

Migtsema   A special prayer of praise and requests to Je Tsongkhapa composed by Manjushri in the *Ganden Emanation Scripture*. The prayer appears in various forms, such as the nine-line and five-line versions. This prayer is very blessed, and those who recite it with faith are able to accomplish great results. See *Heart Jewel*.

Milarepa   (AD 1040-1123) A great Tibetan Buddhist meditator and disciple of Marpa, celebrated for his beautiful songs of realization.

Mistaken appearance   All minds of sentient beings, except for the exalted awareness of meditative equipoise of a Superior being observing emptiness, are mistaken awarenesses because their objects appear to be truly existent; and this appearance is a mistaken appearance that is by nature an obstruction to omniscience. See *Ocean of Nectar*.

Moral discipline A virtuous mental determination to abandon any fault, or a bodily or verbal action motivated by such a determination. See *Joyful Path of Good Fortune* and *Meaningful to Behold*.

Naropa (AD 1016-1100) An Indian Mahasiddha and a lineage Guru in the Highest Yoga Tantra practice of Vajrayogini. See *The New Guide to Dakini Land*.

New Kadampa Tradition – International Kadampa Buddhist Union (NKT-IKBU) The union of Kadampa Buddhist Centres, an international association of study and meditation centres that follow the pure tradition of Mahayana Buddhism derived from the Buddhist meditators and scholars Atisha and Je Tsongkhapa, introduced into the West by the Buddhist teacher Venerable Geshe Kelsang Gyatso Rinpoche.

Non-virtue A phenomenon that functions as a main cause of suffering. It can refer to non-virtuous minds, non-virtuous actions, non-virtuous imprints, or the ultimate non-virtue of samsara. See *How to Understand the Mind*.

Offering to the Spiritual Guide *Lama Chopa* in Tibetan. A special Guru yoga of Je Tsongkhapa, in which our Spiritual Guide is visualized in the aspect of Lama Losang Tubwang Dorjechang. The instruction for this practice was revealed by Buddha Manjushri in the *Ganden Emanation Scripture* and written down by the first Panchen Lama (AD 1569-1662). It is a preliminary practice for Vajrayana Mahamudra. See also *Lama Losang Tubwang Dorjechang*. For a full commentary, see *Great Treasury of Merit*.

Ordinary appearance and conception Ordinary appearance is any appearance that is due to an impure mind, and ordinary conception is any mind that conceives things as ordinary. According to Secret Mantra, ordinary appearances are obstructions to omniscience and ordinary conceptions are obstructions to liberation. See *Mahamudra Tantra* and *The New Guide to Dakini Land*.

Perfection of Wisdom Sutras   Sutras of the second turning of the Wheel of Dharma, in which Buddha revealed his final view of the ultimate nature of all phenomena – emptiness of inherent existence. See *The New Heart of Wisdom*.

Primary mind   A cognizer that principally apprehends the mere entity of an object. Synonymous with consciousness. There are six primary minds: eye consciousness, ear consciousness, nose consciousness, tongue consciousness, body consciousness and mental consciousness. Each moment of mind comprises a primary mind and various mental factors. A primary mind and its accompanying mental factors are the same entity but have different functions. See *How to Understand the Mind*.

Puja   A ceremony in which offerings and other acts of devotion are performed in front of holy beings.

Pure Land   A pure environment in which there are no true sufferings. There are many Pure Lands. For example, Tushita is the Pure Land of Buddha Maitreya, Sukhavati is the Pure Land of Buddha Amitabha, and Dakini Land, or Keajra, is the Pure Land of Buddha Vajrayogini and Buddha Heruka. See *Living Meaningfully, Dying Joyfully*.

Root Guru   The principal Spiritual Guide from whom we have received the empowerments, instructions, and oral transmissions of our main practice. See *Great Treasury of Merit*, *Joyful Path of Good Fortune*, and *Heart Jewel*.

Sadhana   A ritual prayer that is a special method for attaining spiritual realizations, usually associated with a Tantric Deity.

Saraha One of the first Mahasiddhas, and the Teacher of Nagarjuna. See *Essence of Vajrayana*.

Self An I imputed in dependence upon any of the five aggregates. Person, being, self and I are synonyms. See *How to Understand the Mind*.

Sugata A Sanskrit term for a Buddha. It indicates that Buddhas have attained a state of immaculate and indestructible bliss.

Superior being 'Arya' in Sanskrit. A being who has a direct realization of emptiness. There are Hinayana Superiors and Mahayana Superiors.

Superior seeing A special wisdom that sees its object clearly, and that is maintained by tranquil abiding and the special suppleness that is induced by investigation. See *Joyful Path of Good Fortune*.

Sutra The teachings of Buddha that are open to everyone to practise without the need for empowerment. These include Buddha's teachings of the three turnings of the Wheel of Dharma. See *Modern Buddhism*.

Tantra Synonymous with Secret Mantra. Tantric teachings are distinguished from Sutra teachings in that they reveal methods for training the mind by bringing the future result, or Buddhahood, into the present path. Tantric practitioners overcome ordinary appearances and conceptions by visualizing their body, environment, enjoyments, and deeds as those of a Buddha. Tantra is the supreme path to full enlightenment. Tantric practices are to be done in private and only by those who have received a Tantric empowerment. See *Tantric Grounds and Paths* and *Mahamudra Tantra*.

Training the mind 'Lojong' in Tibetan. A special lineage of instructions that came from Buddha Shakyamuni through

Manjushri and Shantideva to Atisha and the Kadampa Geshes, which emphasizes the generation of bodhichitta through the practices of equalizing and exchanging self with others combined with taking and giving. See *Universal Compassion* and *The New Eight Steps to Happiness*.

Transference of consciousness   'Powa' in Tibetan. A practice for transferring the consciousness to a Pure Land at the time of death. See *Living Meaningfully, Dying Joyfully*.

Trijang Rinpoche, Vajradhara   (AD 1901-1981) A special Tibetan Lama of the twentieth century who was an emanation of Buddha Shakyamuni, Heruka, Atisha, Amitabha and Je Tsongkhapa. Also known as 'Kyabje Trijang Dorjechang' and 'Losang Yeshe'.

Truth Body   'Dharmakaya' in Sanskrit. The Nature Body and the Wisdom Truth Body of a Buddha. See also *Buddha's bodies*.

Tsog offering   An offering made by an assembly of Heroines and Heroes. See *Essence of Vajrayana* and *The New Guide to Dakini Land*.

Vajradhara   The founder of Vajrayana, or Tantra. He is the same mental continuum as Buddha Shakyamuni but displays a different aspect. Buddha Shakyamuni appears in the aspect of an Emanation Body, and Conqueror Vajradhara appears in the aspect of an Enjoyment Body. He also said that in degenerate times he would appear in an ordinary form as a Spiritual Guide. See *Great Treasury of Merit*.

Vajradharma   The manifestation of the speech of all the Buddhas. He looks like Conqueror Vajradhara, except that his body is red. There are three ways in which we can visualize him: in his outer aspect as Hero Vajradharma, in his inner aspect as Buddha Vajradharma, or in his secret aspect as Buddha Vajradharma with consort. See *The New Guide to Dakini Land*.

Vajrasattva Buddha Vajrasattva is the aggregate of consciousness of all the Buddhas, appearing in the aspect of a white-coloured Deity specifically in order to purify the negativity of living beings. He is the same nature as Buddha Vajradhara, differing only in aspect. The practice of meditation and recitation of Vajrasattva is a very powerful method for purifying our impure mind and actions. See *The New Guide to Dakini Land*.

Wishfulfilling jewel A legendary jewel that, like Aladdin's lamp, grants whatever is wished for.

Wrong awareness A cognizer that is mistaken with respect to its engaged, or apprehended, object. See *How to Understand the Mind*.

Yoga A term used for various spiritual practices that entail maintaining a special view, such as Guru yoga and the yogas of eating, sleeping, dreaming and waking. 'Yoga' also refers to 'union', such as the union of tranquil abiding and superior seeing. See *The New Guide to Dakini Land*.

Bibliography

Venerable Geshe Kelsang Gyatso Rinpoche is a highly respected meditation master and scholar of the Mahayana Buddhist tradition founded by Je Tsongkhapa. Since arriving in the West in 1977, Venerable Geshe Kelsang has worked tirelessly to establish pure Buddhadharma throughout the world. Over this period he has given extensive teachings on the major scriptures of the Mahayana. These teachings provide a comprehensive presentation of the essential Sutra and Tantra practices of Mahayana Buddhism.

Books

The following books by Venerable Geshe Kelsang Gyatso Rinpoche are all published by Tharpa Publications.

The Bodhisattva Vow A practical guide to helping others. (2nd. edn., 1995)

Clear Light of Bliss A Tantric meditation manual. (3rd. edn., 2014)

Essence of Vajrayana The Highest Yoga Tantra practice of Heruka body mandala. (2nd. edn., 2017)

Great Treasury of Merit How to rely upon a Spiritual Guide. (2nd. edn., 2015)

Guide to the Bodhisattva's Way of Life How to enjoy a life of great meaning and altruism. (A translation of Shantideva's famous verse masterpiece.) (2002)

Heart Jewel The essential practices of Kadampa Buddhism. (2nd. edn., 1997)

How to Solve Our Human Problems The four noble truths. (2005)

How to Transform Your Life A blissful journey. (3rd. edn., 2016)

How to Understand the Mind The nature and power of the mind. (4th. edn., 2014)

Introduction to Buddhism An explanation of the Buddhist way of life. (2nd. edn., 2001)

Joyful Path of Good Fortune The complete Buddhist path to enlightenment. (3rd. edn., 2016)

Living Meaningfully, Dying Joyfully The profound practice of transference of consciousness. (1999)

Mahamudra Tantra The supreme Heart Jewel nectar. (2005)

Meaningful to Behold Becoming a friend of the world. (6th. edn., 2016)

The Mirror of Dharma How to find the real meaning of human life. (2018)

Modern Buddhism The path of compassion and wisdom. (2nd. edn., 2013)

The New Eight Steps to Happiness The Buddhist way of loving kindness. (3rd. edn., 2016)

The New Guide to Dakini Land The Highest Yoga Tantra practice of Buddha Vajrayogini. (3rd. edn., 2012)

The New Heart of Wisdom Profound teachings from Buddha's heart (An explanation of the *Heart Sutra*). (5th. edn., 2012)

The New Meditation Handbook Meditations to make our life happy and meaningful. (5th. edn., 2013)

Ocean of Nectar The true nature of all things. (2nd. edn., 2017)

The Oral Instructions of Mahamudra The very essence of Buddha's teachings of Sutra and Tantra. (2nd. edn., 2016)

Tantric Grounds and Paths How to enter, progress on, and complete the Vajrayana path. (2nd. edn., 2016)

Universal Compassion Inspiring solutions for difficult times. (4th. edn., 2002)

Sadhanas and Other Booklets

Venerable Geshe Kelsang Gyatso Rinpoche has also supervised the translation of a collection of essential sadhanas, or ritual prayers for spiritual attainments, available in booklet or audio formats.

Avalokiteshvara Sadhana Prayers and requests to the Buddha of Compassion.

The Blissful Path The condensed self-generation sadhana of Vajrayogini.

The Bodhisattva's Confession of Moral Downfalls The purification practice of the *Mahayana Sutra of the Three Superior Heap*s.

Condensed Long Life Practice of Buddha Amitayus.

Dakini Yoga The middling self-generation sadhana of Vajrayogini.

Drop of Essential Nectar A special fasting and purification practice in conjunction with Eleven-faced Avalokiteshvara.

Essence of Good Fortune Prayers for the six preparatory practices for meditation on the stages of the path to enlightenment.

Essence of Vajrayana Heruka body mandala self-generation sadhana according to the system of Mahasiddha Ghantapa.

Feast of Great Bliss Vajrayogini self-initiation sadhana.

Great Liberation of the Father Preliminary prayers for Mahamudra meditation in conjunction with Heruka practice.

Great Liberation of the Mother Preliminary prayers for Mahamudra meditation in conjunction with Vajrayogini practice.

The Great Mother A method to overcome hindrances and obstacles by reciting the *Essence of Wisdom Sutra* (the *Heart Sutra*).

A Handbook for the Daily Practice of Bodhisattva and Tantric Vows.

Heart Jewel The Guru yoga of Je Tsongkhapa combined with the condensed sadhana of his Dharma Protector.

Heartfelt Prayers Funeral service for cremations and burials.

The Hundreds of Deities of the Joyful Land According to Highest Yoga Tantra The Guru Yoga of Je Tsongkhapa as a Preliminary Practice for Mahamudra.

The Kadampa Way of Life The essential practice of Kadam Lamrim.

Keajra Heaven The essential commentary to the practice of *The Uncommon Yoga of Inconceivability*.

Lay Pratimoksha Vow Ceremony.

Liberating Prayer. Praise to Buddha Shakyamuni.

Liberation from Sorrow Praises and requests to the Twenty-one Taras.

Mahayana Refuge Ceremony and Bodhisattva Vow Ceremony.

Medicine Buddha Prayer A method for benefiting others.

Medicine Buddha Sadhana A method for accomplishing the attainments of Medicine Buddha.

Meditation and Recitation of Solitary Vajrasattva.

Melodious Drum Victorious in all Directions The extensive fulfilling and restoring ritual of the Dharma Protector, the great king Dorje Shugden, in conjunction with Mahakala, Kalarupa, Kalindewi and other Dharma Protectors.

The New Essence of Vajrayana Heruka body mandala self-generation practice, an instruction of the Ganden Oral Lineage.

Offering to the Spiritual Guide (*Lama Chopa*) A special way of relying upon our Spiritual Guide.

Path of Compassion for the Deceased Powa sadhana for the benefit of the deceased.

Pathway to the Pure Land Training in powa – the transference of consciousness.

Powa Ceremony Transference of consciousness for the deceased.

Prayers for Meditation Brief preparatory prayers for meditation.

Prayers for World Peace.

A Pure Life The practice of taking and keeping the eight Mahayana precepts.

Quick Path to Great Bliss The extensive self-generation sadhana of Vajrayogini.

Request to the Holy Spiritual Guide Venerable Geshe Kelsang Gyatso from his Faithful Disciples.

The Root Tantra of Heruka and Vajrayogini Chapters One & Fifty-one of the *Condensed Heruka Root Tantra*.

The Root Text: Eight Verses of Training the Mind.

Treasury of Wisdom The sadhana of Venerable Manjushri.

The Uncommon Yoga of Inconceivability The special instruction of how to reach the Pure Land of Keajra with this human body.

Union of No More Learning Heruka body mandala self-initiation sadhana.

The Vows and Commitments of Kadampa Buddhism.

Wishfulfilling Jewel The Guru yoga of Je Tsongkhapa combined with the sadhana of his Dharma Protector.

The Yoga of Buddha Amitayus A special method for increasing lifespan, wisdom and merit.

The Yoga of Buddha Heruka The essential self-generation sadhana of Heruka body mandala & Condensed six-session yoga.

The Yoga of Buddha Maitreya Self-generation sadhana.

The Yoga of Buddha Vajrapani Self-generation sadhana.

The Yoga of Enlightened Mother Arya Tara Self-generation sadhana.

The Yoga of Great Mother Prajnaparamita Self-generation sadhana.

The Yoga of Thousand-armed Avalokiteshvara Self-generation sadhana.

The Yoga of White Tara, Buddha of Long Life.

To order any of our publications, or to request a catalogue, please visit www.tharpa.com or contact your nearest Tharpa office listed on pages 301-302.

Study Programmes of Kadampa Buddhism

Kadampa Buddhism is a Mahayana Buddhist school founded by the great Indian Buddhist Master Atisha (AD 982-1054). His followers are known as 'Kadampas'. 'Ka' means 'word' and refers to Buddha's teachings, and 'dam' refers to Atisha's special Lamrim instructions known as 'the stages of the path to enlightenment'. By integrating their knowledge of all Buddha's teachings into their practice of Lamrim, and by integrating this into their everyday lives, Kadampa Buddhists are encouraged to use Buddha's teachings as practical methods for transforming daily activities into the path to enlightenment. The great Kadampa Teachers are famous not only for being great scholars but also for being spiritual practitioners of immense purity and sincerity.

The lineage of these teachings, both their oral transmission and blessings, was then passed from Teacher to disciple, spreading throughout much of Asia, and now to many countries throughout the Western world. Buddha's teachings, which are known as 'Dharma', are likened to a wheel that moves from country to country in accordance with changing conditions and people's karmic inclinations. The external forms of presenting Buddhism may change as it meets with different cultures and societies, but its essential authenticity is ensured through the continuation of an unbroken lineage of realized practitioners.

Kadampa Buddhism was first introduced into the West in 1977 by the renowned Buddhist Master, Venerable Geshe Kelsang Gyatso Rinpoche. Since that time, he has worked tirelessly to spread Kadampa Buddhism throughout the world by giving extensive teachings, writing many profound texts on Kadampa Buddhism, and founding the New Kadampa Tradition – International Kadampa Buddhist Union (NKT-IKBU), which now has over 1200 Kadampa Buddhist Centres worldwide. Each Centre offers study programmes on Buddhist psychology, philosophy and meditation instruction, as well as retreats for all levels of practitioner. The emphasis is on integrating Buddha's teachings into daily life to solve our human problems and to spread lasting peace and happiness throughout the world.

The Kadampa Buddhism of the NKT-IKBU is an entirely independent Buddhist tradition and has no political affiliations. It is an association of Buddhist Centres and practitioners that derive their inspiration and guidance from the example of the ancient Kadampa Buddhist Masters and their teachings, as presented by Venerable Geshe Kelsang.

There are three reasons why we need to study and practise the teachings of Buddha: to develop our wisdom, to cultivate a good heart, and to maintain a peaceful state of mind. If we do not strive to develop our wisdom, we will always remain ignorant of ultimate truth – the true nature of reality. Although we wish for happiness, our ignorance leads us to engage in non-virtuous actions, which are the main cause of all our suffering. If we do not cultivate a good heart, our selfish motivation destroys harmony and good relationships with others. We have no peace, and no chance to gain pure happiness. Without inner peace, outer peace is impossible. If we do not maintain a peaceful state of mind, we are not happy even if we have ideal conditions. On the other hand, when our mind is peaceful, we are happy, even if our external conditions are unpleasant. Therefore, the development of these qualities is of utmost importance for our daily happiness.

Venerable Geshe Kelsang, or 'Geshe-la' as he is affectionately called by his students, has designed three special spiritual programmes for the systematic study and practice of Kadampa Buddhism that are especially suited to the modern world – the General Programme (GP), the Foundation Programme (FP), and the Teacher Training Programme (TTP).

GENERAL PROGRAMME

The General Programme provides a basic introduction to Buddhist view, meditation and practice that is suitable for beginners. It also includes advanced teachings and practice from both Sutra and Tantra.

FOUNDATION PROGRAMME

The Foundation Programme provides an opportunity to deepen our understanding and experience of Buddhism through a systematic study of six texts:

1 *Joyful Path of Good Fortune* – a commentary to Atisha's Lamrim instructions, the stages of the path to enlightenment.
2 *Universal Compassion* – a commentary to Bodhisattva Chekhawa's *Training the Mind in Seven Points*.
3 *The New Eight Steps to Happiness* – a commentary to Bodhisattva Langri Tangpa's *Eight Verses of Training the Mind*.

4 *The New Heart of Wisdom* – a commentary to the *Heart Sutra*.
5 *Meaningful to Behold* – a commentary to Bodhisattva Shantideva's *Guide to the Bodhisattva's Way of Life*.
6 *How to Understand the Mind* – a detailed explanation of the mind, based on the works of the Buddhist scholars Dharmakirti and Dignaga.

The benefits of studying and practising these texts are as follows:

(1) *Joyful Path of Good Fortune* – we gain the ability to put all Buddha's teachings of both Sutra and Tantra into practice. We can easily make progress on, and complete, the stages of the path to the supreme happiness of enlightenment. From a practical point of view, Lamrim is the main body of Buddha's teachings, and the other teachings are like its limbs.

(2) and (3) *Universal Compassion* and *The New Eight Steps to Happiness* – we gain the ability to integrate Buddha's teachings into our daily life and solve all our human problems.

(4) *The New Heart of Wisdom* – we gain a realization of the ultimate nature of reality. By gaining this realization, we can eliminate the ignorance of self-grasping, which is the root of all our suffering.

(5) *Meaningful to Behold* – we transform our daily activities into the Bodhisattva's way of life, thereby making every moment of our human life meaningful.

(6) *How to Understand the Mind* – we understand the relationship between our mind and its external objects. If we understand that objects depend upon the subjective mind, we can change the way objects appear to us by changing our own mind. Gradually,

we will gain the ability to control our mind and in this way solve all our problems.

TEACHER TRAINING PROGRAMME

The Teacher Training Programme is designed for people who wish to train as authentic Dharma Teachers. In addition to completing the study of fourteen texts of Sutra and Tantra, which include the six texts mentioned above, the student is required to observe certain commitments with regard to behaviour and way of life, and to complete a number of meditation retreats.

A Special Teacher Training Programme is also held at Manjushri Kadampa Meditation Centre, Ulverston, England, and can be studied either by attending the classes at the centre or by correspondence. This special meditation and study programme consists of twelve courses based on the books of Venerable Geshe Kelsang Gyatso Rinpoche: *How to Understand the Mind*; *Modern Buddhism*; *The New Heart of Wisdom*; *Tantric Grounds and Paths*; Shantideva's *Guide to the Bodhisattva's Way of Life* and its commentary, *Meaningful to Behold*; *Ocean of Nectar*; *The New Guide to Dakini Land*; *The Oral Instructions of Mahamudra*; *The New Eight Steps to Happiness*; *The Mirror of Dharma*; *Essence of Vajrayana*; and *Joyful Path of Good Fortune*.

All Kadampa Buddhist Centres are open to the public. Every year we celebrate Festivals in many countries throughout the world, including two in England, where people gather from around the world to receive special teachings and empowerments and to enjoy a spiritual holiday. Please feel free to visit us at any time!

For further information about NKT-IKBU study programmes or to find your nearest centre visit www.kadampa.org, or please contact:

NKT-IKBU Central Office
Conishead Priory
Ulverston, Cumbria,
LA12 9QQ, UK
Tel: +44 (0) 01229-588533
Email: info@kadampa.org
Website: www.kadampa.org

or

US NKT-IKBU Office
KMC New York
47 Sweeney Road
Glen Spey, NY 12737, USA
Tel: +1 845-856-9000
or 877-523-2672 (toll-free)
Fax: +1 845-856-2110
Email: info@kadampanewyork.org
Website: www.kadampanewyork.org

Tharpa Offices Worldwide

Tharpa books are currently published in English (UK and US), Chinese, French, German, Italian, Japanese, Portuguese and Spanish. Most languages are available from any Tharpa office listed.

Tharpa UK
Conishead Priory,
ULVERSTON
Cumbria,
LA12 9QQ, UK
Tel: +44 (0)1229-588599
Web: tharpa.com/uk
E-mail: info.uk@tharpa.com

Tharpa US
47 Sweeney Road
GLEN SPEY,
NY 12737, USA
Tel: +1 845-856-5102
Toll-free: 888-741-3475
Fax: +1 845-856-2110
Web: tharpa.com/us
E-mail: info.us@tharpa.com

Tharpa Asia
1st Floor Causeway Tower,
16-22 Causeway Road,
Causeway Bay,
HONG KONG
Tel: +(852) 2507 2237
Web: tharpa.com/hk-en
E-mail: info.asia@tharpa.com

Tharpa Australia
25 McCarthy Road,
MONBULK, VIC 3793, AU
Tel: +61 (0)3 9756 7203
Web: tharpa.com/au
E-mail: info.au@tharpa.com

Tharpa Brasil
Rua Artur de Azevedo 1360
Pinheiros, 05404-003
SÃO PAULO, SP, BR
Tel: +55 (11) 3476-2328
Web: tharpa.com.br
E-mail: info.br@tharpa.com

Tharpa Canada (English)
631 Crawford St.,
TORONTO, ON, M6G 3K1, CA
Tel: (+1) 416-762-8710
Toll-free: 866-523-2672
Fax: (+1) 416-762-2267
Web: tharpa.com/ca
E-mail: info.ca@tharpa.com

Tharpa Canada (Français)
835 Laurier est Montréal H2J
  1G2, CA
Tel: (+1) 514-521-1313
Web: tharpa.com/ca-fr/
E-mail: info.ca-fr@tharpa.com

Tharpa Deutschland (Germany)
Chausseestraße 108,
10115 BERLIN, DE
Tel: +49 (030) 430 55 666
Web: tharpa.com/de
E-mail: info.de@tharpa.com

Tharpa España (Spain)
Calle La Fábrica 8, 28221,
Majadahonda, MADRID, ES
Tel: +34 911 124 914
Web: tharpa.com/es
E-mail: info.es@tharpa.com

Tharpa France
Château de Segrais
72220 SAINT-MARS-
 D'OUTILLÉ, FR
Tel/Fax : +33 (0)2 43 87 71 02
Web: tharpa.com/fr
E-mail: info.fr@tharpa.com

Tharpa Japan
KMC TOKYO, JP
Web: kadampa.jp
E-mail: info@kadampa.jp

Tharpa México
Enrique Rébsamen Nº 406,
Col. Narvate Poniente,
CUIDAD DE MÉXICO,
 CDMX, C.P. 03020, MX
Tel: +52 (55) 56 39 61 80;
 +52 (55) 56 39 61 86
Web: tharpa.com/mx
E-mail: info.mx@tharpa.com

Tharpa New Zealand
2 Stokes Road, Mount Eden,
AUCKLAND 1024, NZ
Tel: +64 09 631 5400
DD Mobile +64 21 583351
Web: tharpa.com/nz
E-mail: info.nz@tharpa.com.

Tharpa Portugal
Rua Moinho do Gato, 5
Várzea de Sintra,
SINTRA, 2710-661, PT
Tel: +351 219231064
Web: tharpa.pt
E-mail: info.pt@tharpa.com

Tharpa Schweiz (Switzerland)
Mirabellenstrasse 1
CH-8048 ZÜRICH, CH
Tel: +41 44 401 02 20
Fax: +41 44 461 36 88
Web: tharpa.com/ch
E-mail: info.ch@tharpa.com

Tharpa South Africa
26 Menston Rd., Dawncliffe,
Westville, 3629, KZN,
REP. OF SOUTH AFRICA
Tel: +27 31 266 0096
Web: tharpa.com/za
E-mail: info.za@tharpa.com

Index

The letter 'g' indicates an entry in the glossary

S

Further Reading

If you have enjoyed reading this book and would like to find out more about Buddhist thought and practice, here are some other books by Venerable Geshe Kelsang Gyatso Rinpoche that you might like to read, or listen to. They are all available from Tharpa Publications.

HOW TO TRANSFORM YOUR LIFE
A Blissful Journey

A practical manual for daily life that shows how we can develop and maintain inner peace, how we can reduce and stop our experience of problems, and how we can bring about about positive changes in our lives that will enable us to experience deep and lasting happiness. This is a significantly revised edition of one of Venerable Geshe Kelsang's most popular and accessible books.

For a free eBook of *How to Transform Your Life* please visit www.howtotyl.com.

MODERN BUDDHISM
The Path of Compassion and Wisdom

By developing and maintaining compassion and wisdom in daily life, we can transform our lives, improve our relationships with others and look behind appearances to see the way things actually exist. In this way we can solve all our daily problems and accomplish the real meaning of our human life. With compassion and wisdom, like the two wings of a bird, we can quickly reach the enlightened world of a Buddha.

For a free eBook or PDF of *Modern Buddhism* please visit www.emodernbuddhism.com.

HOW TO UNDERSTAND THE MIND
The Nature and Power of the Mind

This book offers us deep insight into our mind, and shows how an understanding of its nature and functions can be used practically in everyday experience to improve our lives.

The first part is a practical guide to developing and maintaining a light, positive mind – showing how to recognize and abandon states of mind that harm us, and to replace them with peaceful and beneficial ones. The second part describes different types of mind in detail, revealing the depth and profundity of the Buddhist understanding of the mind. It concludes with a detailed explanation of meditation, showing how by controlling and transforming our mind we can attain a lasting state of joy, independent of external conditions. Also available as an eBook.

JOYFUL PATH OF GOOD FORTUNE
The Complete Buddhist Path to Enlightenment

We all have the potential for self-transformation, and a limitless capacity for the growth of good qualities, but to fulfil this potential we need to know what to do at every stage of our spiritual journey.

This book offers a detailed explanation of the entire path to enlightenment, with the teachings of Buddha laid out step-by-step making them very easy for the modern reader to put into practice. A perfect guidebook to the Buddhist path.

'This book is invaluable.' *World Religions in Education.*

THE ORAL INSTRUCTIONS OF MAHAMUDRA
The Very Essence of Buddha's Teachings of Sutra and Tantra

This precious book reveals the uncommon practice of Tantric Mahamudra of the Ganden Oral Lineage, which the author received directly from his Spiritual Guide, Vajradhara

Trijang Rinpoche. It explains clearly and concisely the entire spiritual path from the initial preliminary practices to the final completion stages of Highest Yoga Tantra that enable us to attain full enlightenment in this life. Also available as an eBook.

THE NEW EIGHT STEPS TO HAPPINESS
The Buddhist Way of Loving Kindness

This inspiring book explains how we can transform all life's difficulties into valuable spiritual insights by meditating on one of Buddhism's best-loved teachings, *Eight Verses of Training the Mind* by the great Tibetan Bodhisattva, Geshe Langri Tangpa. The author reveals practical ways in which we can use this timeless wisdom to find meaning and lasting happiness in our busy modern lives. Also available as an eBook.

'... induces calmness and compassion into one's being.' *New Humanity Journal*.

THE NEW MEDITATION HANDBOOK
Meditations to Make our Life Happy and Meaningful

This popular and practical manual allows us to discover for ourselves the inner peace and lightness of mind that comes from meditation. The author explains twenty-one step-by-step meditations that lead to increasingly beneficial states of mind, and that together form the entire Buddhist path to enlightenment. Also available as an eBook.

'This manual provides a succinct and inspiring overview of the many ways in which Buddhism can be applied to the situations and activities of daily life.' *Spirituality and Health*.

To order any of our publications, or to request a catalogue, please visit www.tharpa.com or contact your nearest Tharpa Office listed on pages 301-302

Finding Your Nearest Kadampa Meditation Centre

To deepen your understanding of this book, and other books published by Tharpa Publications, and its application to everyday life you can receive support and inspiration from qualified Teachers and practitioners.

Tharpa Publications is part of the wider spiritual community of the New Kadampa Tradition. This tradition has a growing number of centres and branches in over 40 countries around the world. Each centre offers special study programmes in modern Buddhism and meditation, taught by qualified Teachers. For more details, see *Study Programmes of Kadampa Buddhism* (see pages 295-300).

These programmes are based on the study of books by Venerable Geshe Kelsang Gyatso Rinpoche and are designed to fit comfortably with a modern way of life.

To find your local Kadampa centre

visit: tharpa.com/centres